March 1958.

The
School
in our
Village

books pp28-29
pp57-65
p69
p77
p80
pp88-9
p96
pp101-107

THE SCHOOL IN OUR VILLAGE

by

Joan M. Goldman

Illustrated by Edward Ardizzone

LONDON

B. T. BATSFORD LTD.

First published, 1957

PRINTED AND BOUND IN GREAT BRITAIN BY
JARROLD AND SONS LTD, LONDON AND
NORWICH, FOR THE PUBLISHERS
B. T. BATSFORD LTD
4 FITZHARDINGE STREET, PORTMAN SQUARE,
LONDON, W.1

CONTENTS

Abridged excerpts from this book have appeared in THE TIMES EDUCATIONAL SUPPLEMENT *and the* EVESHAM JOURNAL

EARLY DAYS

N the year 1900 a new school was built in this small, secluded Cotswold village, the old one being considered "unsuitable for a place of learning".

It was not deemed unsuitable for a private dwelling house and, as such, has been occupied ever since. Its sham-Gothic windows are now curtained, but the tower that held the school bell is still there (though the school bell is not).

This—by contemporary standards—humble edifice faces the "new" school across a wide expanse of village green, known as the Common, which is on the summit of a hill several hundred feet above sea-level.

Though the later school shames the earlier one by its appearance, it is, contrasted with schools built in the last decade, itself inadequate, but a closer acquaintance with it reveals advantages that

9

to some extent atone for its narrow windows and absence of central heating.

These advantages are best defined as being of the "homely" sort strictly missing in large city schools. Everything, from schooling to school dinners and medical inspections, takes place in a large, lofty hall that is the school, and in here, on chilly mornings, the village children customarily spend a few moments warming their hands and chatting in front of the open fire before school officially begins. It has much the air of a comfortable and well-ordered living-room, an impression accentuated by the two glass doors which lead off from it, respectively, to the kitchen (where the school dinners are cooked daily) and the cloakroom.

We are fortunate in having recently had the room tastefully refurnished with the "latest" school furniture in the shape of light tables and chairs, blackboards on wheels and gaily painted movable cupboards. The tables, dotted about here and there informally and not in any kind of standardised formation as in the old type of school, are bedecked perpetually with small pots of flowers, leaves or berries that the children are encouraged to bring; and once a week a lively fifteen minutes is given over to polishing the woodwork of the tables until it literally reflects the fresh country faces of the little polishers.

Conditions naturally were not always so in even this "new" school. Instead of the sixteen children of Primary age who now comprise the Register there were at the beginning of the century something like seventy-two children crowded into this same hall for their schooling. The age range varied from three to thirteen years, and in addition to the head teacher—for the most part uncertificated—there worked an uncertificated assistant and a young person described as a monitor. From these three, functioning in a room forty-four feet long and fourteen feet wide, was dispensed education as the country child knew it.

Accompanying the ordeal of overcrowding were oil lamps, bucket lavatories, and heavy, iron-legged desks each holding six children as though in a vice. No Burnham Scale existed to attract the ambitious teacher to country teaching. The records tell us that the headmistress's salary in 1900 was seventy-five pounds per annum, her assistant's salary thirty-five pounds per annum, and the monitor's twenty pounds per annum. Even remembering the cheaper cost of living in those days, economically—whatever her "social" pretensions—a teacher's status was about on a par with the more impoverished type of costermonger. Some teachers make a similar complaint today.

Undeniably, however, whatever the setbacks and obstacles, country teachers in those days, who can be rightly described as being among the pioneers of Primary education where the practice of it is concerned, energetically persisted in trying to maintain what standards they could in a community where education was not, as it is in today's average community, a sought-after prize. During harvests the older children would be absent from school for as long as nine weeks at a stretch; and there were other enticements for their time such as cider-grinding and potato-lifting—not to speak of the severe weather conditions that so often kept the not-well-nourished younger children house-bound. Outbreaks of scarlet fever, diphtheria and other infant scourges would also deplete school numbers to the extent sometimes of forcing the place to close for as long as two or three weeks during the epidemic.

In face of all this you can't help admiring when, on reading the records, you continually encounter evidence of a teacher's determination to ignore contemporary discouragement and to persist in outlining scheme after scheme for "raising the scholastic standards". One's own task today seems so light in comparison.

Inspectors' reports preserved from those days are illuminating, not least in the type of bureaucratic language then in vogue. One inspector recommends that "a musical instrument would be a useful addition to the tuning fork now in use": in plain words, a piano. It arrived—ten years later.

Illuminating in a different way is the entry by an inspector in the Log Book in beautiful copperplate handwriting: *I this day paid a surprise visit to the school, but found the Register in order.*

The inspector is probably now dead, but in that entry one almost *hears* his disappointment ringing down the years.

What of the "scholars" (as the teacher invariably, and picturesquely, refers to them in the Log Book)?

It appears to have been the usual aim of the village family whose child attended school to obtain for him at the age of twelve a Labour Certificate enabling him to leave school and become what the Labour Certificate describes as "beneficially employed". The sequel would be work on one of the surrounding farms in the case of a boy and service in one of the big houses in the case of a girl.

For those failing the examination (consisting of a certain modest proficiency in the 3 R's) schooling continued till the age of fourteen.

To glance at the "Schemes of School Work" drawn up by the headmistress of those days is to sympathise with the mass of children straining to escape to a farm at the age of twelve. There is nowhere even the hint of a desire to include in these "schemes" subjects—or even a subject—of the sort that can evoke a spontaneous growth in the classroom.

In the year 1901 the teaching of poetry (recitation, they called it) consisted of going systematically, and collectively, through a "suitable" book, and memorising from it forty lines a week. "Uplifting" poems—*Excelsior*, *The Slave's Dream*, *The Village Blacksmith*—were exclusively in favour.

Written English, equally rigid in its technique and making no call on the child's imagination, consisted of "the formation of simple sentences" in the case of the lower Juniors and "simple letter-writing" in the case of what were defined as "the more advanced scholars".

"Dictation", "Copy Books", "Transcription" complete the scheme-of-work where the subject of English is concerned.

Handwork was apparently non-existent apart from drawing: for this subject were needed "models and pictures suitable for the object lessons".

Artistic horizons widened by 1904 to include "chalk-drawing from memory".

In arithmetic one set of "Code Requirements for Standards I–VII" covers the needs of the whole school. Whatever these "Code Requirements" were they sound a very far cry indeed from the intricate, particularised, practical arithmetic schemes of our own day.

The "tone" of all these early schemes-of-work is, without a single exception, what we would today call dour and down-to-earth. Successive headmistresses complain incessantly of the wide age range in this school, and the trials of teaching everybody at the same time in a room where only a thin, movable partition divides the "Upper Division" from the "Lower Division". In one year early in the century a headmistress baulked at accepting three-year-olds in school, and in the Log Book threatened: "If mothers say they are busy and send their children to school with their older brothers or sisters, then I shall send them home again."

Her successor to the headship relented of this measure, but complained that "the little ones do disturb the bigger scholars".

There was additionally the problem of the mentally defective children for whom, far more hopelessly than today, no suitable school could be found. The headmistress in 1917 writes, with undisguised exasperation: "Mary Y was examined. . . . She is to remain at school and I am simply to amuse her."

It was the years which followed World War I that brought the first really noticeable changes to this little village school. Education can at this stage be described as beginning to "look up", although teachers' salaries did not achieve a similar elevation, and the lady who did the school cleaning in 1920 is recorded as receiving the intoxicating wage of two-and-sixpence a week for it.

However, education itself was undoubtedly "looking up". In 1921 domestic science as a subject reared its head in the curriculum, and the Senior girls were taken once a week to the nearest market town on a one-and-a-half-mile tramp for "the privilege", as the Log Book terms it, of there imbibing the mystic rites and ceremonies endemic to the aforesaid subject.

In the same eventful year a gentleman representing something called "The Choice of Employment Office" visited the "top standard". What, however, really made the year memorable was the historic act of laying on water in the school. It must be added that it was unfit for drinking, and did not extend its favours to the bucket lavatories, but it is only fair to urge on the credit side that for the first time in the school's history children could be sent out of the classroom to wash. Possibly the local die-hards shook their heads at this new-fangled gadget when only a short time after its installation the school had to be closed down for two days on account of someone having left the tap running all night and flooding the school. . . .

By 1926 this all-age school had become a Junior and Infant establishment, as it remains today, and the numbers on the roll had whittled down to forty-two, forming two classes for a headmistress and her assistant. The iron-legged desks that seated six had given way to iron-legged desks that seated two. The playground, hitherto an enclosed piece of village common, and nearly impassable in the winter when great blizzards blow across here from the distant hills, was asphalted.

An element of mild geniality—or humanity, for those who prefer the word—was seeping into the existing methods of teaching. Whereas in 1901 the headmistress had recorded: "A boy brought some live mice to school which afforded some amusement for a few minutes until I deemed it fit to send the boy home with them," there are in 1926 and afterwards records of tadpoles being reared as frogs in school. Officially, also, a school garden flourished. Slowly the influence of the pioneers in contemporary methods of teaching was making its mark on the minds of the humblest units in the profession. Inspectors, once obsessed with "time-tables", are now recorded as urging "more freedom in the Infant room".

This new freedom, once encouraged, brought with it an entirely new orientation in teacher-pupil relationships. The kind of teacher "horror-struck" at the child who tells a lie—and what child doesn't perpetually do so?—became a comic figure of the past; and was joined by those other solemn bigots that the nineteenth century produced in such proliferous numbers who believed that bad language or unpunctuality in an infant automatically earned him a place among the eternally damned.

Above all, the cane ceased to be, like the gallows a century earlier, arbitrarily depended on as the tried and trusted remedy for social misbehaviour. As a consequence, the teacher herself was in many instances becoming more of a guide and friend for the children and less "the schoolmistress".

A long, arduous, tortuous process has been this slow emancipation of the small village school from its beginnings as "an institution for the education of young people". *Institution* is perhaps the operative word here!

I would like to show some indication of the current achievements in schooling that this emancipation, whose processes are still on the move, has brought to the children in our country Primary schools.

ALONE

AFTER occupying my post here for some months I was asked by the Education Committee to arrange for the three oldest boys in my school to be transferred to the Junior boys' school, one and a half miles away in our local market town. It was considered preferable for them at the age of nine to attend a larger school for two years as a prelude to being transferred at the age of eleven to the local Senior bilateral school. The headmaster of the Junior boys' school happened to have some vacancies, and the additional advantage that a school bus passed the village in the main road at the bottom of the hill clinched the move.

Their disappearance brought down the school numbers from

nineteen to sixteen, and I asked myself, as a growing number of people who are not teachers are asking: "Is there any point these days in a one-teacher village school?"

My own collection ranged from a large, shy, unbelievably quiet girl of ten called Amy to a tiny, under-sized, highly strung boy of five called Willie.

Their school has recently been lavishingly equipped with the most tasteful modern furnishings, a full-time cook prepares dinner for them each day on the premises, and although it is only a *Group O* school my own salary is by no means a negligible item in the school's expenses. I could not help recalling the days not so long before when for less money I taught a class of fifty children in a big city school; it made me wonder whether then I was not, from the State's point of view, more profitably employed.

My sense of guilt was sharpened when the boys who were to be transferred to the Junior school came to take their leave of me. One of them, whose eagerness had understandably got the better of his tact, said: "It'll be nice going to a real school, Miss!"

No one could mistake what he meant: a football team to join, cricket in the summer, a gymnasium, the pride of belonging to a "House" and the incentive to help make it "top".

My initial sympathy with their release from a restricted world to entry to that of a big one was tempered by doubts when I looked again at the little group that had remained in my keeping. Knowing each one so well, I could see them in my mind's eye being helplessly shipped off to augment various swollen class-rooms in the event of my school closing down: the image was not comforting.

I thought of Amy, my single ten-year-old pupil, a girl so reserved in temper that even after five years' attendance at school she has to summon goodness knows what resources of moral courage to address teacher. I thought of Bernard, seven and a half years old, whose uncontrollably noisy response to anything that disturbs the routine of school life could so easily be misinterpreted in a large class in a large school and inevitably bring punishment. I thought of Lily, an enchanting little doll of a girl aged five who, attending the same school with an older brother and sister, feels so secure, but who, pushed out somewhere on her own, would I am sure close up like a clam.

No doubt they would eventually "manage" in whatever school they found themselves, but I am not anything as sure that they would at the same time remain the natural, unspoiled beings that they are here.

For the nine-year-old boy the drawbacks in a village school are perhaps unarguable. Most normally healthy boys of this age are straining to be off into the rough and tumble of life, and though the needs of most girls in this direction are less urgent many of them would be better off for the change. It is the age preceding for which there are some powerful arguments for the retention of the small village school as an "institution for the education of the young".

Not that it is, from teacher's point of view, the easiest place from which to dispense the desired education—despite the deceptive air of leisure that lies about it. I have worked harder here than at any of the congested city schools I served, and for the simple reason that whatever the children learn or do not learn lies solely at my door. I do not feel I can be casual and then explain away its depressing results by the time-honoured edict much favoured in my profession: "The Junior school's methods are hopeless—our Infants always seem backward when they get there."

Here both Infants *and* Juniors are my responsibility, and I am sufficiently fresh to the post to experience an occasional flash of panic during which I am suddenly convinced that I shall never teach the Infants to read or induct the Juniors into the mystery of decimals. In this fleeting nightmare I see myself as a creature trapped in the limelight of a public shame: she who took all that Burnham offered and gave naught in return . . . but the mood passes and reading and decimals are once again under precarious control.

Worries of this sort are, I suppose, the concomitant of a position held in isolation. Except for an occasional inspector and a passing word or two from a parent the teacher has no contact with adults in her working day.

This is not quite as grim as it sounds, for after all there are only sixteen children to think about, and the hustle and bustle indivisible from the running of a large city school classroom are here unknown. There is nevertheless a certain sense of strain in the knowledge that one is as it were holding the fort in a tiny but vital outpost in our far-flung educational empire. I can honestly say that I have never tried to ease this strain by permitting the children a single minute more of playtime than the rules allow, on even the sunniest afternoon, or spent—head teachers please note!—a moment more than is strictly necessary chatting to inquiring parents. Not to uphold this standard in a one-teacher school would bring down on one a consciousness of guilt that could not be nullified by the leisure stolen or the gossip enjoyed. It's a self-discipline comparable to the legendary dressing for dinner in the jungle: it involves extra work, but it keeps up one's morale.

On my acceptance of the post here, I inquired: "What happens if I am ill one day?"

The answer? "Just telephone the office and close the school until we can get a supply teacher out to you."

It sounds very simple, but I doubt if any teacher in such circumstances would take advantage of it with an untroubled conscience. I myself—like most teachers, I imagine—have carried on during those rare occasions when I have been attacked by a headache, cold, or bad throat—excepting one single Monday in the year when a high temperature, added to the rest, forced me to bed.

Mrs. Duckworth, the cook-cum-cleaner, a solid and resolute woman who finds illness and death incentives for heroism, promptly damped down the school fires, cancelled the milk, closed the canteen and took it upon herself to inform every child's mother personally of the catastrophe. It takes absurdly little to whip up excitement in a village, and a day's illness on the part of "the Governess" (as some of the old inhabitants describe me) was much more than that little. I don't know what speculations or prognostications were aired at the supper table or in the pub concerning my illness, but when I turned up hale and hearty next day there was a kind of subdued disappointment about the place. Though wishing me no harm, a little more complexity and drama in my illness would have been preferred. It had been too prosaic. Even worse: it had been too short. I believe Mrs. Duckworth spoke for the village when she commented: "You should have had another day or two in bed, at least."

The village—it can at this point be stressed—is one of the most important factors contributing to the small school's "otherness" in contrast to the city school. Almost everyone who lives here has been a pupil in my school. The older inhabitants have watched headmistresses come and go and it gives them the feeling, understandably, that the school is theirs rather than the headmistress's. Teaching methods, they realise, may change, but through it all, come what may, there stands their school, indestructible seemingly, like their church and pub; it's a part of them. A headmistress, sensing this and sensing also that there probably surrounds her person an atmosphere redolent of big towns and alien influences, will never succeed in quite shaking off the feeling that the village is watching her and is specially watching to see what she is doing with this particular bit of its tradition.

It must bring to teaching and living in the village where one teaches a set of problems that can surely exist nowhere else. The headmistress is at one and the same time a part of the community, and yet separate from it. The goodwill of the village is a help to her work, and yet she will often be in the position of having to insist on standards of behaviour that may well clash with immemorial custom. She will need to bring fresh vigour and new ideas into the school, and yet often have to summon miraculous resources of patience to cope with the slow pace of her progress or even with a kind of passive opposition to it.

Her battle will not be limited to pupils or parents. A far more dour struggle will often take place inside herself in the attempt to maintain her customary interest in, and energy for, the larger educational world and its doings in the face of personal isolation and surrounding indifference. It's so easy—it's even tempting—after the first careless rapture of settling into the place, and with the first year's work behind one, to go "native". Who, you may ask yourself, cares or even knows what you are doing? Inspectors are rare visitors, keen young student teachers are rarer—why should they come all this way when a single stride brings them within reach of a city school?—you have no staff with whom to discuss problems as these arise. For the greater part of the year there is You and nothing but You.

For this reason alone lectures, conferences, informal gatherings of the educational clan—tortuitous travelling though attendance involves—is a vital part of one's teaching life in a village.

Education authorities do, in many cases, attempt to arrange transport for teachers from rural schools who, without possession of a car, would find it impossible to attend functions. In our local market town there are often courses and discussion groups arranged for teachers from the surrounding villages. These can help a teacher to retain a sense of feeling part of a corporate body with which she can share, if not always identical opinions on methods of teaching, some of the more general aims of the profession. It can be comforting, and sustaining, to learn that other teachers in other villages have problems and difficulties similar to one's own which, granted the happy occasion, can even perhaps be solved in harness.

More headmistresses might also make use of their "Occasional" holidays to take a peep into a rural school that they have never seen before. There are many more of these places than would be suspected which are doing unusual and interesting work, and a day's inspection of one could be as stimulating and thought-provoking as a whole course of lectures.

More than any other kind of school the one-teacher sort in a highly industrialised country such as ours will depend for its vitality and usefulness on the official in charge of it. Though this has always been so, it must be remembered that for the good, bad and indifferent school of the past there was no alternative schooling for the country child; whereas now, with so many large and efficient schools within easy distance of most villages—what my ex-nine-year-olds call "a real school"—becoming increasingly available year by year the country parent is likely in ever-growing numbers to do some hard thinking in the choice of school for his child, with consequences that may not always leave the reputation of the village school unimpaired.

My contention is that a well-run village school, once its natural shortcomings and special problems have been faced and surmounted, can make a unique and necessary contribution to education in a mass-production society such as ours.

JUNIORS AND INFANTS

 RECALL myself at the age of seven attending what was then called an Elementary School and being caned for persistent late-coming.

It was by no means my first encounter with this system of punishment and it did not perturb me unduly. Had I instead of it been asked, "Why are you late?" and had I felt like answering truthfully I should have replied on these lines: "Because I have made up a game called 'Fairies and Giants', and I play this game on the way to school and it has a way of delaying me."

So enamoured was I of this game that for several weeks I could not forgo it, and had in consequence to endure several canings.

I imagine—or shall I say I hope!—that it must be a long time since a child in an Infant department in any Primary school has been caned for whatever reason; possibly there does not now exist a school where even Juniors are caned for unpunctuality. Most teachers would—or should—be more concerned with the reason or reasons that make a child late for school than with the act of his lateness.

Such a child attends my school: a seven-year-old boy called Henry. Regularly at some time between five and fifteen minutes past nine in the morning he lurches into school, heavy-eyed, bewhiskered by the remains of his breakfast and without any pretence that he would not rather be back in bed.

I do know that Henry does not go to bed early enough at night. I also suspect a contributory cause like anaemia in accounting for his lethargy, and I am therefore not harsh with his unpunctuality.

Unhappily for Henry there are others beside me in the school who can tell the time, and Henry's transgression is noted darkly by some of his virtuous classmates. To add to his troubles there is Eric.

Eric is a big, good-looking boy of nearly nine. He is not only the biggest boy in the school but the eldest and, there being no man on the premises to keep an eye on things, Eric has taken it upon himself to do so. He enjoys the responsibility, but is not so absorbed in it as to overlook the compensating privileges (invented by Eric and not conferred on him by me). One of these "privileges" is for him to offer me, occasionally, with well-intentioned deference, advice on how to run my school.

He is firmly of the opinion that, for a start, I am too easy on other people's shortcomings (though naturally not on Eric's!), and as he is one of the first to arrive at school in the morning he has no welcoming mat out for Henry when he turns up a good half-hour afterwards. He greets Henry's entrance with the announcement: "Just look at the time!"

Henry, hardened to public shame, continues to try to slip unobtrusively into his seat.

If I say nothing to Henry, Eric follows up the heavy hint with a blunt accusation: "Henry's just come and it's ten past nine." He adds, in case my mental arithmetic is not all it should be: "He's ten minutes late."

If I still ignore Henry, Eric tells the boy next to him in a stage whisper that's as effective as a proclamation to the whole school:

"She'd jolly soon grumble if we were late. She makes *us* come early."

He knows this to be untrue, but unless he pretends that usually I am cross with late-comers he will have no case against Henry; and in the cause of making a case against Henry, truth, as he sees it, is expendable. He identifies himself with my authority and feels that "our" position is undermined by Henry's casualness. He treats me as though I am a Prime Minister approaching my dotage and he my confidential secretary who must, for reasons of personal loyalty and the nation's good, keep a steady hand and eye on the affairs of state.

Outside these encounters with Henry the two boys' relationship with each other is amicable enough, as also are those between Eric and the other children. It is simply that he has the urge to make his opinion felt from time to time, and this is very natural, for he is older and far more schooled than the rest. All that's necessary is for one to be on the watch to ensure that such a boy does not bully the rest. It's inevitable in a small group of this kind for one or two of the older ones to invariably take the lead in organising games, acting as unsolicited spokesman for the rest and, with the egotism inseparable from childhood, to do all they can to dominate their fellows.

They may be—they often are—apart from this perfectly likeable and friendly children and, what's more, apt *not* to find themselves at all natural leaders in a larger group that they may subsequently enter; but in a school like mine, with sixteen on the roll, there is faint likelihood of competition for such as Eric, and he becomes a kind of unauthorised head boy simply by virtue of his size and energy.

So familiar a situation is this in the small school that it is perhaps worth while to consider how best to deal with it. The most effective way, I should think, is to attempt to guide so much of Eric's energies to good use that little will be left for bad use.

Not that I would subscribe to a policy of leaving him in charge of the children on occasion. This can make the others feel that you look on him as a kind of "pupil teacher"; it must result in consolidating his power over them. This applies not to Eric alone but to any Junior who, given half a chance, will exult in acting the policeman over the little ones.

My own solution in the case of such a boy is to incite in him a sense of "helpfulness". Eric, for example, is at present occupied, outside his lessons, in trying to teach five-year-old Doris how to tie bows in her shoe-laces. Initially his attitude was: "Fancy not being able to tie a bow!"

Those odd moments in several of the past days spent in attempting to teach Doris the knack have taught him in the process the valuable lesson that tying a bow can be a genuinely complex task for a five-year-old and that we are not born the resourceful creatures we later find ourselves to be. Because he is experiencing her difficulties together with her he now appreciates them.

Similarly with ten-year-old, silent Amy: her own problem of inarticulate shyness is eased by her being encouraged to read stories to the Infants. Though it is unlikely that the Juniors would hear her out in patience—or she find the confidence to attempt to read to them—the little ones cause her no blushes or breakdowns.

There are more ways than can be counted of satisfying the natural feelings of superiority in Juniors while at the same time employing them usefully.

In a corner of the hall is a large Wendy House. The older children have decorated it with *appliqué* curtains, have painted its dresser, have embroidered a table-cloth for it, baked salt-and-flour cakes for the "tea parties" held there, modelled and painted clay ornaments for its interior, and have even affixed an imposing knocker to the front door.

Another example.

Older children take it in turns to "lead" Morning Assembly. I play the hymns on the piano but otherwise take no part. The

Juniors seem to love this ceremony and unfailingly, in every case, conduct Assembly with almost a fierce earnestness.

When it came to Mavis's turn I was rather perturbed. She is a girl of eight with a reading age of five and a half. She is big, stolid but friendly, and works extremely hard at reading. At the start of this innovation I had impressed it on the Juniors to write out their own prayers on the evening preceding the morning they were to deliver them—and not fall back on the prayers that *I* habitually use when taking Assembly.

When it was Mavis's turn she came to me and said:

"I shall get our Mum to teach me my prayer, then I shan't have to read it from a paper."

Next morning she stood before the school with eyes closed, hands folded in reverence, and uttered the following words:

"Dear God, thank You for all good things. Please take care of us through the day and help us to do our lessons and learn to read. Amen."

One unintended by-product of the Prayers was the differences in personality brought out by the readings.

Arthur, the only child in the school of Eric's age, who is a rather scatter-brained lad, perpetually seized by the most improbable of grandiose schemes that never come to anything, handed us this as his contribution to Morning Assembly:

"If God wants to do anything, He can do it. I wish we could have enough boys in this school to make up a football team. Then we could play the Church school and I bet we would beat them. And I wish we could have school colours like the Church school does, and I should choose red and white because that's the colours of the Arsenal. Amen."

Following this, I suggested that Prayers might conceivably consist in future of other things besides blatant demands for something. In a burst of virtuousness Eric called out: "I bet God thinks it ever so greedy when you just keep asking for things all the time." Actually Eric's own prayers have sometimes had a decided taint of the acquisitive, but I let it go.

Next day a boy called Peter, aged eight, showed how he had profited from Eric's maxim.

Peter is a quiet, under-sized boy undisguisedly anxious to please those in authority. He has a knack of being able to look pious without the least effort. While the rest stood with bowed heads he read in a high, fluty voice:

"Our Father which art in Heaven, You are very good and You give us all good things. We must not be greedy and ask for things. And Jesus is good, too. I go to Church on Sunday and help the Rector give out the hymn books. Please look after us all the time. For Jesus's sake. Amen."

Another of our methods in inciting initiative is the appointment for a term at a time of a class librarian.

Library books are loaned on Friday and returned either on the same day or on the following Friday. The librarian arranges his books according to subject-matter and labels each section. We own a rubber stamp with the date on it and can keep a record of borrowed books.

Everyone belongs to the library; the smallest children borrow picture books. The librarian is responsible for simple repairs to books. He attends to them in odd bits of free time in school or at home afterwards. He chooses a book at the end of term to keep as payment for his services.

As a result of a recent grant of money for reading books from the Education Committee I was able to take the three eldest children to help me choose some books in the bookshops of a large near-by city. Each child picked out the biggest and most picturesque books on the principle presumably that bigger books are better books and, as this is sometimes the case, the plan worked well. Our list included books by Edward Ardizzone, Père Castor, Jean de Brunhoff and that charming anthology of poems, *Stars and Primroses*, by M. C. Green.

When I asked Eric his reason for choosing this last book he smiled in embarrassment, hesitated and said: "I dunno . . . I liked all that different kind of writing in it and the way it's all in different colours. It's not like an ordinary book."

The adventure of buying books is not, of course, a frequent one, and it is therefore necessary to be constantly thinking up new ways of conferring extra responsibilities on the eight-and-upwards Junior child. I try to remember all the time that a school such as mine is as much a kind of family as anything else, a family with the older members playing an increasingly important role in it.

A girl like large, silent, ten-year-old Amy, whose instinct leads her to slide away out of sight to the back of the class, benefits greatly from the rarity of children as old as herself: it ensures that there will be certain duties that she, and only she, must undertake. She serves the younger ones at dinner. It's she who unlocks the cupboards in the morning before school begins. On Mondays she sits beside me at my desk and collects the dinner-money and National Savings, and it s this of all her activities, I believe, that gives her most pleasure. She has little to say about it, but she feels —I sense—a pride in my confidence in her to handle "real" money. The fact that I sit beside her while she does it in no way minimises her pride in the task; and, strange to relate, slow as she is in ordinary written arithmetic, she has never yet made a mistake in the dinner and savings moneys: a record I can't, alas, claim for myself.

I have written at such length about Junior children here because the twin problem of responsibility and power belongs far more to them than to the Infants.

What can result, of course, is a tendency of Infants to acquire the habit of "leaning" on Juniors, of enlisting their help only because they are all in the same classroom in an atmosphere of ease and freedom. As most Infants delight in independence the danger mentioned is unlikely to be widespread; but instances will always exist. Ours is Willie, aged five and a half, an only child, highly strung in the extreme and abnormally babyish in behaviour, though not so in his intelligence.

He cannot put on his outdoor clothes, he cannot change his shoes for Physical Education, he cannot carry anything for more than a yard without dropping it. Though I say cannot, *will not, if help is available* is a more accurate definition of the difficulty.

As he is a boy whose instinct on meeting an obstacle is to burst into tears one's own instinct is to beckon someone like Amy or Eric or Mavis and say: "Would you put Willie's coat on him, please?" or "Do fasten Willie's shoes", or "Take these building bricks to Willie's table, would you?" And in some such way the job is done in two minutes with no fuss. Everybody is happy, including Willie (or should I say *especially* Willie?).

The method's one drawback is that it is disastrous for Willie's character; so at present we are putting up with tears and tantrums from Willie—who obviously doesn't give a rap that it-is-for-his-own-good—as he puts on his coat upside down or inside out, pokes his right foot into his left shoe and can't get it out again, spills beads, that he has been threading, all over the floor on his way with them to the cupboard. To Willie in these moments I seem to be a-woman-without-a-heart; but his torment is forgotten in a rush of pride when the task has been rightly achieved and in a panting lisp he boasts: "I did it meself, Miss."

I pat his head and murmur: "Good boy. I knew you could."

THE DAY BEGINS

Y cook-cum-cleaner, Mrs. Duckworth, lives in a small cottage overlooking the school playground and divided from it by a roadway nine feet in width. She has been keeping the school clean for thirty-three years. Headmistresses have come and gone, but like Tennyson's brook Mrs. Duckworth seemingly goes on for ever.

She recalls as though it were yesterday the headmistress who, thirty years before me, ate raw cabbage for her lunch, and her successor to the headship whose husband publicly sold meat in Mrs. Duckworth's front room that she calls the parlour. When asked by me how this unusual arrangement had come to pass she replied: "Well, he wanted to set up in the butchering trade," as if this explains how he and his meat joints came to be a fixture amongst her best furniture.

Intimacy of this kind with numerous head teachers has given Mrs. Duckworth a kind of proprietary air towards school and education. Having "cleaned up" after generations of village school children she views the occasional worldly ambitions of some of their parents with a sceptical eye and is fond of telling me at odd times stories of parental fecklessness with money poured out unprofitably on dull offspring.

There was, for example, a little dumpy girl whose parents' pretensions landed her into a local "school for ballet", but who now resignedly works in the woollen mills a mile down the road (not as a ballet dancer, needless to say). Another child, a boy with mildly prosperous parents, was sent early on to a private school at eight guineas a term and, although he is now a grown man, has nothing to show for his "education" but a conspicuous disinclination for work. In Mrs. Duckworth's words: "They just can't get him out to work. He won't do a stroke."

It should be made clear at this point that there are many in the world who could take up ballet or walk about, in Mrs. Duckworth's phrase, "like a gentleman"—and earn Mrs. Duckworth's approval in doing so; but her prosaic neighbours and their offspring do not qualify for this exercise of her charity. Having herself to get up in rain or shine at six-thirty of a morning to sweep the school and light the fires she has little patience with those "in no better station", as she puts it, who hanker after a more "refined" existence. She started her working life in service in one of the big houses so plentifully dotted about the countryside in the early days of the century, and the relatively rigid social arrangements between the different classes then existing won for ever her admiration. She feels that people bred in humble circumstances should remain humble and backs it up with the additional maxim that "hard work never killed anybody". Had the art of public speaking been among Mrs. Duckworth's many talents she would be a Force that the Labour Party could ignore only at its peril.

Certainly if her own life is anything to go by she is undoubtedly, at sixty-three, a strong, well-set-up woman whose services are utterly dependable. By the time I am brewing my first cup of tea in the morning I can see from my windows on the opposite side of the school playground the smoke rising from the tall school chimney, and know that Mrs. Duckworth has been at work for a solid hour, and that I shall find the school, when I enter it, as warm as toast on even the bitterest winter's day.

I cross into school at about twenty minutes to nine. Mrs. Duckworth will already have left it at eight-fifteen, but with the main door open so that those children who wish to come early may not be impeded in this urge. This could not easily be arranged in a big city school, but it is certainly practicable where a small group of children are involved, and it is a pleasant beginning to the day for the children to know that as soon as they are ready for school, school is ready for them.

A bell-rope, unused by me, hangs at one end of the school hall. "If you pull it," the children told me in expectation of seeing my eyebrows shoot up in incredulity, "it makes the bell ring."

That is what happened in my predecessor's time at five minutes to nine every morning: a signal for the children who had often been waiting for a long time to tumble into school from the playground. Since some of them like to appear at about twenty minutes past eight, it has seemed to me an unnecessary procedure, and worse than unnecessary on winter mornings, to have their childish spirits regulated by a school bell.

The first to arrive are usually my oldest boy, Eric, and his near-contemporary, Arthur. They bring into school the school milk standing in the playground, chalk up the new day's date on the blackboard, and then occupy themselves with an activity of their own choice.

Soon ten-year-old Amy arrives in school. She unlocks the cupboards, puts out the exercise books and generally makes the place ship-shape for the coming day's work.

Each Junior has a diary which he fills in daily and illustrates, so early arrivals of this sort have plenty to do until school officially commences. It usually lasts them, in fact, until just after nine o'clock.

Meanwhile, in the first few minutes of the official day I am busy with the four five-year-olds who sit together at two small tables. They share a communal News Sheet which they take it in turns to fill. Thick, black pencils are used for it. I try if possible to introduce the elements of number into their "news" so that the activity is virtually a kind of 3 R's.

Typical entries read:

> Willie played at marbles with his Daddy. He has 6 marbles. 2 are red, 3 are green, and 1 is blue.
> Doris brought daffodils to school. There are 5 daffodils. They smell nice.
> Colin's dog has 3 puppies. Their eyes are still closed. How many eyes will open soon? 6 eyes.
> Lily is 5 today. She has a cake with 5 candles on it. She is going to have a party.

Each page is illustrated with a large picture drawn and coloured by the children with either pastels or paint. The completed thing is hung on the wall like a calendar, the top page carrying the heading in large coloured letters: DAY BY DAY.

It hangs low enough for them to read it without strain, and they find a pleasure in turning back to the pages already inscribed and proudly reading them to anyone who cares to listen or who is by chance within earshot. Should the meaning of the words they have written slipped their memory the drawings are there to serve as a reminder.

I feel that with very young children a link between home and school should be maintained, particularly by means of an invitation to mothers to come and look at the child's work. As the children may enter school before it officially begins nothing is easier than for Mother to accompany them and spend a few minutes in the classroom being thrilled by her child's progress, and thrilling the child by her praise of it.

Only small numbers in a school can permit intimacy of this

kind, but where it can be managed it seems to me to have a happy effect on the school's atmosphere.

By about nine-fifteen the diaries are completed and the last of any visiting mothers has departed. Only Friday is an exception to this custom. On that day parents are invited to Morning Assembly.

Fathers are not usually available, and there are mothers for whom it is equally inconvenient to attend; but the invitation is there, and some parent or other is invariably present to make use of it.

The service is quite short: two hymns, a prayer and a Bible reading delivered by one of the Juniors. It helps to create, I like to believe, the feeling in the children that school and home are not, like work and home, utterly disparate things. It helps to create this feeling in the parent, too, I hope; a feeling that, once rooted, can be an essential contribution to the well-being of any school, large or small.

I have taught in schools where visiting parents are, like those in hospitals, treated by the staff as a kind of necessary evil. They are regarded as a disintegrating influence on routine, it is assumed (not without cause) that they are exclusively on the watch to see that *their* child gets the attention they think it merits, they are unrestrained in their gossip with one another about the faults they find with the school, and in general if you don't keep them at bay you will soon not be able to call the school your own. This, approximately, is the way The Profession views parents.

I know a large Primary school in the centre of one of our foremost industrial towns on whose front gate hangs the notice:

Parents are not allowed beyond this gate unless they wish to see the Headmaster.

Such is the reputation of the headmaster in the locality that it would indeed take a reckless parent to set foot over the threshold for any reason that could be even doubtfully interpreted as frivolous. There is a flavour of the nineteenth century about this school notice, harking back to the days when the Primary school was for so many children a forerunner of the reformatory, and when so many parents of such children looked upon the teaching staff as warders and the headmaster as the "Governor".

This sometimes led to a situation—again resembling prison procedure—where a parent who regarded his child as a victim of injustice would take it upon himself (and even more frequently *herself*) to right matters by invading the school to wreak vengeance on some harassed and perhaps overstrict teacher.

Such a situation is today, happily, almost as far distant from the realms of possibility as would be a resuscitation of Dotheboys Hall and its horrors. Particularly do I feel this when I see the so-anxious-to-please mothers of my own children joining with us in *All things bright and beautiful* on a Friday morning.

For the youngest children it is a keen delight to have Mother with them at school for a few minutes once a week, and if for some reason Mother is not available a grandmother or grandfather will often deputise. Children not yet of school age come within this privilege if the parent of an older child already at school wishes to bring them along on these occasions. It helps the pre-school child to become familiar with the school's premises and its routine, so that when its own time comes for school the break with home will not be as sharp as it often is elsewhere.

A handicap in a small village school is the rarity of visitors. It's another reason for parents being welcomed to call. Both children and teacher have a very natural urge to show strangers what they are doing, to as it were achieve an audience, to reap the benefits of helpful criticism. No village school can hope for as much as it would like to have of this kind of thing. Here, the constant interest of parents and their relations is an undoubted and unmixed stimulus.

For example: we have a small cloakroom where the children, on entering school, hang their outdoor clothes before proceeding into the hall. For us who make use of this annex the activity is an ordinary one; but the knowledge that visitors will pass through the place when calling on us is an incentive to keep it clean and gay. The walls are decorated with children's paintings, including a startling contribution by Peter, aged eight, of a giant snake. This work is his particular sequel to a book entitled *A Child's Book of Snakes* that I gave him to read one afternoon. Beneath it he has written something that might be more accurately defined as a warning than a description. It reads:

This is a cobra. Very poisonous. It is the largest poisonous snake in the world.

Peter is by nature a retiring type of boy and vastly enjoys, in contrast to his usual humble lot, the attentions bestowed upon him by virtue of the surprise to visitors of the "specimen" on the cloakroom wall that meets their eyes on entry. No explorer who had actually brought that cobra back alive could carry about him an air more redolent of quiet, self-confident courage than does young Peter who merely painted it. It even impressed the censorious and gently patronising Eric, who told him: "I reckon that's one of the best paintings in this school." This made Peter breathe hard through his nose in precariously restrained pride. He knew that praise could come no higher. . . .

Besides the paintings there is a large calendar with an appropriate picture for each month in the year—the work of the Juniors —and I try, whatever the season, to have flowers, leaves, buds or berries brought to school and placed in pots on the cloakroom as well as the classroom window-sills.

Immediately the children arrive in school in the morning they change the water in the pots, arrange any flowers they may have brought and print an appropriate label on a card to stand beside the particular pot. I take it to be important for the children to feel themselves responsible for maintaining the school's fresh and pleasant appearance, and to be encouraged in whatever art there is in flower and leaf arrangement.

Plain glass jam-jars make excellent pots for holding exhibits, and have an additional advantage over fancy vases in that plain glass leaves the stalks visible. I also think it worth while for the children to save their pennies from time to time to buy an interesting piece of pottery; but care must be taken that however small the pottery purchased it is attractive. Pots and vases should never, I feel, be accumulated regardless of their appearance. Children ought to be shown that the most attractive bouquet can be ruined by presentation in a hideous vase.

This "fussiness" with vases can occasionally lead to trouble. There was that memorable bright summer's day when Mrs. Duckworth cast a critical eye on my collection of gleaming jam-jars and fish-paste pots: memories of the workhouse, as derived from a reading of popular Victorian fiction, must have risen unbidden to Mrs. Duckworth's mind, and she accordingly arrived next day with two of the most appalling examples in the way of vases I have ever seen. I found them on my table on entering school. One was a plaster model of a girl with a hole in her head for the water and stalks, the other was of the kind popular in cemeteries, a dark green in colour and squat in shape.

"They'll do to be going on with," was Mrs. Duckworth's introduction to the gift in words pregnant with threat.

What could one do but use them?

At first I slipped them into the most unobtrusive places, but regularly I found them resettled on the most conspicuous shelves that Mrs. Duckworth regarded as deserving of the honour. There was no alternative for me but to accidentally break one: the plaster girl with the hole in her head.

The cemetery vase I could not even break on purpose. Like the memory of those it is constructed to venerate, it is imperishable. "Nor marble nor the gilded monuments of princes shall outlive" it. I have it with me still.

THE 3 R'S: *ARITHMETIC*

I WAS once a young assistant teacher to the headmistress of an Infant school in Birmingham who had adopted Free Activity. We practised it from nine to ten each morning, and settled down afterwards with a sense of relief to the "real" day's work.

I thought of Free Activity in those days after the style of that legendary parent who had made a similar distinction between ordinary school work and what she thought of as "intelligence", which resulted in the following request to her eleven-year-old son's headmaster: "As he is so near his scholarship exam., could he have your permission to drop history and geography and take intelligence instead?"

Yes, I thought of activity as a "subject" in the school curriculum and the hour given over to it each day as a kind of glorified handwork lesson. Had I been asked: "What do you think the term Free Activity means?" I think I should have answered: "I think it means what it seems to say: that the children are active and that they are free to choose in which way they shall be active."

I might have followed this definition with a demonstration of a classroom of children playing with Plasticine, looking at picture books, painting, occupied with a hammer, nails and bits of wood, weaving with raffia and cutting out pictures. I would have been hoping in a benevolently vague way that after an hour of this "freedom" the class would be better fitted to cope with the ordinary school lessons.

I was lucky, subsequently, in being able to visit several Primary schools where activity methods were more imaginatively interpreted, and to talk with teachers for whom Free Activity was not a subject to be fitted into an overcrowded time-table but the essence of a *general approach* to education.

From that moment I became a supporter of the principle— though not, I should add, an unquestioning supporter of it. I do, however, regard it as perhaps the best of all approaches to education in a one-teacher school such as mine.

How then does Free Activity in a one-teacher school vindicate the claim I am making for it as probably the best method available?

To make clear where I stand, let me say at once that I look upon it as the primary duty of a Primary teacher to teach children the rudiments of the 3 R's. An efficient teacher should take that in her stride and manage much else besides; but the 3 R's are the first essential. No teacher is justified in larking around with arty-crafty business at the expense of the 3 R's no matter what "dramatic" results she can dig up from it for the titillation of some jaded inspector. If Drama is what *she* wants to produce and *he* wants to see, the 3 R's, believe it or not, can be made to satisfy both.

In my school I have at one age-end ten-year-old Amy, soon

due for the Common Entrance Examination, and at the other end five-year-old Colin who counts up to ten like this: 1, 2, 3, 4, 6, 8, 11, 5, 10, and who is as happy to read words backward as forward. He tries to read them forward when I ask him to, but he thinks it is a whim on my part, and that in humouring it he is putting me in his debt.

Between these two children are fourteen others at various stages of development, all demanding all the individual help they can get. The abiding problem in a one-teacher school is how to make a homogeneous unit of this raggedly formed regiment.

My own solution is to give each child as much chance as is possible to work at his own pace and to work at a subject of his own choice.

Arithmetic occupies us every morning until 10.30 a.m. From 9.40 until then written and practical arithmetic over as wide a range as possible is being pursued in every part of the school hall.

The Infants do no formal written arithmetic. Any sums they may do spring solely from their practical work. Both they and the Juniors have each a book called *It's Fun Finding Out* and into that book go all scraps of number knowledge. In it eight-year-old Mavis, who baked a cake at home and was permitted by Mother to weigh out the ingredients single-handed, wrote from memory both the recipe and her method of cooking it. She then learned from an equally obliging village storekeeper the cost of her ingredients, and compared it with the cost of buying a similar cake in a shop. She was delighted to discover a saving of ninepence on the home-made version. "And I bet it tastes better, too," she said. "Our Mum says you never know what they put in shop cakes."

There is Bernard, seven and a half years old. He is the eldest but one in a large family, and such personal possessions as rarely come his way are, understandably, treasured. He was given a box of dominoes at Christmas. He first used them for building bricks and devising little "houses" dotted around the table. When this palled he tried balancing as many dominoes as he could on top of one another. After exhausting this and similar forms of play with the dominoes, and finding himself unable to think up further variations, I showed him how to play what we adults call "a game of dominoes".

He has an inadequate understanding of number and tries to keep away from having to encounter it if he can. I suggested that he try a game with me. He did, and won. This excited him rather and he drew in his number book a diagram of the completed game, colouring his own dominoes red and mine black. "If anybody wants to know how to win at dominoes," he advised the children at the neighbouring tables, "they can look at this picture."

At the very bottom of this age-scale comes Colin. As with the other five-year-olds, his book contains only the simplest number discoveries which at this stage are closely linked with the writing of English.

We have a large toy "stationer's" shop in school that the children have made themselves. It figures much in their writings. Colin had woven a simple paper mat to be sold in this shop and he wrote in his book: "6 strips of paper. That makes a mat." He drew a picture of it, too, of course.

Sitting by him is Willie, also aged five. Willie, as hinted elsewhere, is an intelligent but extremely excitable little boy. He writes his letters and numbers so fast and with so little care that it's nearly impossible to read them. When he is finished he lets his pencil drop with a clatter on the table, from where it invariably rolls on to the floor, and announces at the top of his voice: "Done!"

His favourite activity at present is the use of scales, but since his instinct provokes him to strew the floor around him with whatever quantities of sand, horse chestnuts, acorns or cowrie shells have been put at his disposal, a very watchful eye has to be kept in his direction.

He does not bother with weights, but tries to balance both bowls on the scales. He has discovered as a result that ten horse chestnuts are equal in weight to a small bag of sand—and similar monumental phenomena. These are complex operations for him and he feels a keen sense of achievement when he finally sees two bowls hovering on a level with each other without catastrophe.

When he called over for me to come and witness this—
chestnuts versus sand—I took the chestnuts and placed them in a
bag and let him hold that and the bag of sand in his hands to feel
their weight. Left alone, I don't think Willie would make written
records of his experiments in a book, but I think even the smallest
children should be encouraged to do this; for as "practical arithmetic" is not, or should not be, a lesson set apart from written
arithmetic, the making of notes as the child goes along is all-
important.

With the older children the practical application of the number
rules they learn is substituted for the Infants' learning-through-
doing.

My two eldest boys, Eric and Arthur, have measured the height
of everyone in school, and were then set by me the task of
finding the difference in height between different children. They
measured me, and Eric—who prefers those in authority to look
the part—experienced a twinge of grief on discovering that I was
only one and a quarter inches taller than ten-year-old Amy.

From there they took to measuring the height of the classroom
door. Arthur then made the comment that he knew a man who
had to bend to enter the kitchen in Arthur's house. I suggested
that he measure his kitchen door that evening. On discovering
subsequently that it measured six feet one inch, he made the
approximate deduction on the following morning that the family
visitor would measure about six feet two inches in height.

There is in school a weighing machine that is used by the local
doctor on his visits. We have tried using it ourselves, and it seems
to give the children an odd sense of the "reality" of those things
called stones and pounds when we find, for example, that Willie
and five-year-old Doris weigh together exactly as much as does
Eric alone.

A positive orgy of weighing and measuring followed this
discovery; so much so that someone summoned the temerity to
request Mrs. Duckworth, our cleaner-cum-cook, to try the scales.
This is where Mrs. Duckworth drew the line. She delicately
divulged to me later: "I'm over twelve stone." I couldn't help

thinking, wistfully, how impressed Eric would have been to see this, with his own eyes, on the scales.

Another enjoyable activity is for children to devise problems for other children to solve. Edith, Bernard's six-and-a-half-year-old sister, is a bright, lively girl whose tiny feet are securely planted in reality. A problem she devised went as follows:

> Sixteen children are cleaning their teeth. Nine have bleeding gums. How many have not?

Henry, our seven-year-old lethargic latecomer, puts into arithmetic some of the energy he forgoes using in life:

> A fierce bull chases ten boys. The bull can't catch Henry, but he catches all the others and tosses them on his horns. Can you tell how many he tosses?

It's odd how children set about working out these gruesome "problems" with a keenness they would never muster for the old, far less alarming If-a-tap-and-a-half-fills-a-bath-and-a-half type of problem.

Ten-year-old Amy can tell the time and, because of it, thought she knew all there is to know about the details of a clock face. I said to her one day: "I wonder if you can teach Bernard to tell the time?"

I gave her a large wooden clock face with movable hands, and listened to how she went about teaching Bernard to tell the time. It was a crucial test of her knowledge of English as well as that of her arithmetic to make such an attempt. For a whole fortnight she gave five minutes of every day to this task, as a result of which Bernard can now tell the time. It incited him to ask: "Who taught people to tell the time a long time ago, I mean before they had clocks?"

This gave rise to a discussion on the lines of a short history of clocks. It was soon plain to the children themselves how intimately time-telling is connected with the movement of the sun. We found out that someone in the village had a sun-dial and permission was obtained from him to inspect it. The older children made primitive hour measurements with water dripping through a pin-sized hole in the bottom of a metal bowl. The side of the bowl was marked to indicate the amount required to last an hour.

Similar experiments, such as testing how much of a candle will burn away in an hour, are performed, and the details of it recorded in writing. It struck me about some of the children that they would willingly, even joyfully, have consented to the breakdown of all the clocks in their homes for the chance of installing their own substitutes.

This relating of number to everyday living is not always easy to organise among large masses of children, but I view it as the essence of the meaning of practical arithmetic, and a one-teacher school is ideal for its application. Children are so crammed full of unasked questions that it would be a pity not to coax some of these out of them to be used as a basis for number experiences, rather than limit the children to text books—bright and gay as these might be in appearance. In consequence there will not be those neat exercise books with their numerous rows of sums and tiny ticks of approbation in the margin to show an awed visitor; but is he missing much?

I recall being proud of these excessively neat "sum books" in my first days as a teacher of seven-year-olds; until a visiting inspector, on being shown them, said to me: "You could train an intelligent monkey to do this kind of thing."

He softened the blow by recommending a certain course of lectures on "Number in the Primary School" which, when I subsequently attended them, persuaded me of how far removed from even an elementary grasp of arithmetic is the mere doing of "sums". A child may successfully work out on paper innumerable sums involving the four rules in Number and yet, when questioned orally, supply the following answers:

Question: How old would you say your father is?
Answer: I don't know. He said he's twenty-one.
Q.: Do you think he is really twenty-one?
A.: Yes.
Q.: Is he a big man or is he small and thin?
A.: Oh, he's a big man.

Q.:   How heavy would you think he is?
A.:   Well ... (*after hard thinking*) he could be about a ton.
Q.:   How heavy are you?
A.:   I forget.
Q.:   Could you guess how tall your father is?
A.:   Well ... (*hard thinking again*) about ten feet.
Q.:   This room is ten feet high. Is he as tall as this room?
A.:   (*Laughing*) Of course not.
Q.:   How tall is he, then?
A.:   Three feet.

That's the way it goes. You would say: here is a boy who has no conception of age, weight, measurement; yet his exercise books are chockful of sums correctly answered, and the prospect of working on his own with a text book brings him no worry.

Take an ordinary eight-year-old girl in a Primary school for questioning on her knowledge and understanding of what she has learned. This, like the other, is of course a true-life example. She has for some time been working on addition and subtraction of hundreds, tens and units with carrying figures; and there seem to be no mistakes in her work.

Q.: Here is a box full of matches. I shall empty all the matches into my hand. How many matches would you guess there to be?
    (*The girl begins to count them.*)
Q.: No, don't count them. Just guess.
A.: (*Worriedly*) Twenty.
Q.: I shall take half the matches. There. Guess how many are left?
A.: There should be only ten, because that's half of twenty. But there's ever such a lot more than that.
Q.: Guess how many?
A.: I don't know.
Q.: Five hundred?
A.: (*Smiling*) Oh, no.
Q.: Perhaps only five?
A.: No.

46

Q.: Well?

A.: (*Shaking the head*) I don't know. I couldn't tell without counting them.

Q.: Shall I tell you? There are now thirty left. So how many did we have at first?

A.: (*Blushing*) Oh, that's easy. . . . Sixty.

This is a girl quite at home with numbers in the abstract, yet is far from being truly fitted for the written work she is actually doing when she has so vague a conception of numerical values.

Arithmetic is a most difficult subject among difficult subjects to teach, and one must be constantly on the watch for those children who race ahead in it without grasping anything of its essence. Not constant instruction but constant experiment is in my view the best method for the best results.

THE 3 R's: *WRITING*

'AS t' go 'ome straight arter school."

"Doan marrer. I allus comes wiv yer, anyway."

"T'ain-no-good comin' ternight. I stops in of a Fridee and watches Telly."

This is how most of my children talk to each other; it's how they talk to me, too, except when a raised eyebrow sends them scurrying into their "best" speech, which is painfully slow and crippled by errors.

My first introduction to the written word, as it is handled locally, was a note from the father of one of my boys:

Dear Miss

i wishes to tell you as my boy will not be in the school for a fornit as i as my holidiy from the works and the mother and i is taking him out to his grans and oblige yours . . .

Shade of Miss Nancy Mitford. . . .

Where exactly, I asked myself, do I begin the historic task of inducting them in the art of expressing themselves in their native tongue in a manner that will not entirely disgrace it?

I could have tackled it in the traditional way: text books, set exercises, lavish red-pencillings of their errors. I decided this would not get us very far; for the crucial drawback to text-book English, as so many of my disheartened colleagues could testify, is that it stimulates no urge in the child to write or speak well.

We all know the child who writes out twenty sentences with a capital letter at the beginning of each sentence and a full stop at the end of it; and we all know the teacher who says "Good!" and marks the exercise with twenty ticks. The child feels mighty pleased with himself, but where will it get him when he sits down to write a letter or a composition, unaided? Oh, he knows in theory all about the capital letters and the full stops, and he knows that if he gets them in the right places "Miss" will be pleased, and that if he doesn't "Miss" will frown and perhaps call him a fool; but does he know what he is doing and why he is doing it?

Very often not.

Worse, this hit-or-miss method of writing English may, in the average or dull child, destroy utterly any chance there may have been for him to enjoy the business of writing English. These tiresome little exercises result in either sending him into a flurry whenever he puts pen to paper or, as exemplified by the father who wrote me a note, make him think there are so many rules that he might as well ignore the lot and be done with it.

Yet even the dullest child—surely?—has his thoughts, ideas and day-dreams and would delight, granted the power, in the opportunity to express and convey them in speech or writing.

Of all the children in my school perhaps ten-year-old Amy, the eldest, is the "slowest". She has an I.Q. of eighty-five, and gives an impression of not so much enjoying childhood as merely somehow getting through it!

I suggested to her one day that she write something about her elder brother. Anxious always to be no trouble to anyone, she set to work and filled two pages with descriptions of her brother on these lines:

> He works on the roads and in the evening he plays darts with me. He has a dog and he takes it for walks sometimes. He has a young lady and he goes to her on Sunday.

It was all right, but so dull.
I asked her: "How old is your brother?"
"Eighteen."
"Do you get on well with him?"
A nod.
I persisted: "No squabbles?"
A slow smile spreads across her face: "Sometimes."
"What do you squabble about?"
In Amy's reply there was a note—hitherto unknown—of emphasis: "He likes his own way too much."
"Go back and write about that," I suggested.
A little later she returned with this paragraph added to her story:

> People are always saying he's a quiet boy, but they don't know him and he is ever so bossy and he always likes to win at darts. My mother says he'll have to alter when he's married. I think he is a nuisance and I expect he thinks I am a nuisance, too.

Some of the spelling was very poor and the punctuation is better not described, but I said nothing of this to Amy because the important thing in my view was that for the first time she was telling in words what she thought and felt instead of squeezing out of herself a dull recital of "facts" which had told me nothing about her brother. Only the last few sentences, crudely though they may have been expressed, had begun to bring him to life.

This, if any kind of advance is to be made in the teaching of English, is the first essential: the release in the child of pent-up ideas and a confidence in him encouraged to give them utterance.

I always allow my children to say what they wish to say in

writing in their own way. I would never cramp their style for the sake of a grammatically immaculate result. I don't mean that I ignore or gloss over bad writing; I mean that the teaching of grammatically correct English is only a part of the business of teaching English and that this is more easily achieved when a child is himself impatient to take up a pen and express his thoughts.

For this reason part or all of the period between eleven and twelve each morning, and sometimes part of the afternoon as well, is given over to what my children call "story writing". They write stories based on their everyday lives, or imaginative stories, or stories—retold in their own words—that they have read or heard from me, or whatever other form they wish to choose for the exercise.

As they are children whose lives do not teem with incident I do what I can to remedy this in the limited ways that suggest themselves.

Even a visit to a local farmer milking his cows or one *to* us from the local constable to talk on road safety stimulates new thoughts and a new vocabulary to express them. Inspectors, school managers, the man who comes to read the electric meter: all are grist to our literary mill.

The younger children mostly content themselves with a brief description, accompanied usually by a bold painting of the subject. One of these subjects was our rector whose semi-sombrero type of headgear occupied in nearly every picture more than half the space. It must have made an impression. . . .

The older children are beginning to savour the delights of a more subtle assessment of character or appearance.

Kate, eight and a half, wrote about the small brown terrier brought into school by a visiting inspector one morning:

> I have felt his head and when you touch it, it is like the new mat we use for P.E.

As the new mat is of coconut matting, Kate certainly had a point there!

Peter, also eight and a half, our best reader—and, it would seem, observant to boot!—wrote of me:

> If you do something wrong she doesn't always grumble at you, but she blames you with her eyes.

Their stories of "imagination" are not, understandably, anything like as penetrating. Making up stories is for them at present almost the equivalent of learning to speak a new language.

I never set them a subject. Whoever is straining to get off his chest some horrific saga of spacemen or spies is free to do so.

This type of story varies from the simple sort attempted by lethargic, seven-year-old Henry: "One day I am going to kill a giant," to an attractively compiled booklet written and illustrated by ten-year-old Amy which describes the sad adventures of an orphan girl in search of a home. Amy shares with Mrs. Duckworth, the cleaner, a weakness for what one might call the darker side of life, and she wrote of the trials and tribulations of her heroine with noteworthy gusto.

This little book of hers took a week to complete; but how much more profitable and pleasurable a week than one thrown away on English exercises and corrections; and how much more she had learned at the end of it! She had given of her best handwriting, pen drawings executed in coloured inks with immense care and, withal, a watchful eye kept open for errors in English that no amount of set work could have incited in her.

Not least, she had discovered in herself something never before felt: confidence. Nor is she alone in the discovery. There is growing among the pupils a slow but surely discernible conviction that life and language are not disparate—let alone warring —entities.

I think this was brought out by the Juniors when they wrote playlets for the glove puppets they had made.

At the performance of one of these the youngest children formed the ideal audience. The very sight of the puppets and the sound of the Juniors talking in "funny" voices sent the Infants off into peal upon peal of laughter. One play which particularly won their favour was the work of that painstaking, eight-and-a-half-year-old reader of ours, Mavis.

She comes from a home where matrimonial bliss is not all that, according to the weekly passion papers, it should be; and Mavis's "inspiration" draws deeply from this fount. One of her plays centred on a quarrel between a husband and wife on account of the husband refusing to sit in with the baby and leave his wife free to attend "the dance". This was the dialogue:

Wife: Just because you can't dance you think nobody else should.
Husband: Dancing! That's all you think about.
Wife: I shall get our Dad to deal with you, you mean old thing.
Husband: If he comes here I shall hit him over the head.
  (*Wife in a frenzy then attacks husband and a kind of Punch-and-Judy take-off follows.*)

Though this is not, admittedly, in the best-that-has-been-thought-and-felt tradition in the theatre, it does have an encouraging effect in our own little humble circle; and that is something for a start.

Mavis could not have written this playlet without vast help from me, for her ability to read and write is retarded; but even granted the help, the result being a snippet of her own that other children could read and act—and which could provoke the laughter of appreciation—was for Mavis a tremendously exciting experience that was a definite encouragement to her in her struggle with the written word.

Fast on the footsteps of this new-found interest in the act of writing sprout up other interests connected with it.

Full stops, for example, have for some reason taken seven-and-a-half-year-old Beryl's fancy. I think she is still inclined to see their function as decorative rather than useful, and she likes displaying them prominently in her work; but it is better than ignoring them as mysteries too dangerous to tamper with.

The Junior section, venturing further, is becoming conscious in general of the need for inverted commas on occasion. Eric, our unofficial "Head Boy", ever in the vanguard of a new movement, had asked me the purpose of the exclamation mark. When I explained it as an additional emphasis to a sentence regarded by the author of it as particularly important, Eric—who regards the lightest of his own utterances as all-important—began from then on to hand me work in which you couldn't see the words for the exclamation marks . . . but over-enthusiasm is undeniably preferable to indifference.

This section might be fittingly concluded with an extract or two from the diaries of some of the children. (The diaries, it should be remembered, are uncorrected.)

From Peter, aged eight:
We went down the village to play with Henry. We played cow-boys. Henry and I were bandits. Eric had a stage coach. We got Eric and tied him up and I shot him. I cut the rope. Then he got me and took me to his camp and shot me. Then Henry got me away. Then we threw boxes at each other. Then I went home and had my tea and got some apples for my mother.

From Arthur, nearly nine:
I played with Eric and we climbed up a tree with a ladder and he gave me some stones to drop down so that we could play the Dam Busters. It was a good game. Then some big kids chased us and we ran home.

Arthur (on another day):
I played cowboys outside and I pretended to shoot my cat. The cat ran away. When I was in bed my cat came up on my bed and bit my hair.

Bernard, seven and a half:
Last night I played in the road with my sledge and when I was sliding the men came round with the grit. Then I could not slide, so when the men went I got the grit off the road.

Henry (the unpunctual one) economises on his energy but makes his point:
I have a lot of sweets at home and I keep them safely in the larder. My sister can't have them. They are mine.
Last night I played with a lot of kids. We were warring each other and fighting.

I had a pancake and a half for my tea. Then I got down from the table and got the lemon and squirted it in my mouth. Our Mum hit me.

The girls' diaries are rather different in tone.

Susan, seven:
Mummy went to Sunbury and bought me some new knickers. They have pictures of cats and dogs on them.
One day I was born in the hospital. I was our Mum's baby and she called me Susan.

Mavis, eight:
Yesterday I played with Amy. We played with her dolls. She has got a doll about 3 feet tall. She has a suit case full of dolls' clothes.

Edith, six and a half:
It is pancake day and I am going to have 2 pancakes. I shall have sugar on them. I will eat them up very fast. We are going to have orange juice on them. Daddy will make them because Mummy is in hospital. She is getting our new baby from there. Daddy has got to do all the work now.

Elizabeth, six years:
I have a brother named Peter. He has a blackboard. He writes on it. He wears black trousers and he is little. He helps Daddy to get some water for our birds. He talks to the birds in the cages. He chases me with his gun.

Each day's entry is illustrated by any medium the child cares to choose. I try to allow opportunity for as much interplay as possible between the making of pictures and the written record they adorn. Sometimes the drawing (or painting) comes before the writing and helps to release ideas that might otherwise die unrecorded.

Edith, six years old, one day painted a picture called "My Family". It was a lively portrait, and when she got to the stage of expressing the same idea in words they did not belittle her illustration to them:

I have 3 brothers in my house. John, Bernard, and Leslie. Only Bernard comes to this school. Bernard is naughty because he makes a noise in bed. Mummy says, "Don't make a noise because Leslie is asleep." John just sits in a chair to read his book. He is too lazy to help Mummy. I am a good girl.

What strikes me chiefly about such writing is the pleasure so evidently gained in its execution. I think most teachers would agree that to make a child *want* to write is to half-win the battle before it is joined.

The joy involved in this for country children is especially a keen one, for the notion of filling whole notebooks with what goes on inside their simple souls is novel and provocatively flattering. To quote "Head Boy" Eric who (like Confucius) has his comment for all occasions:

"We are surrounded by stories in this school."

I might have rejoined: "You are surrounded by your teacher's efforts to make you write and speak good English"—but I don't think it would be wise to let him or the others into the secret!

THE 3 R'S: *READING*

ETHARGIC little Henry was accompanied to school by his mother on one of his late mornings. The time was nine-twenty: a good ten minutes beyond the point of his usual latecoming, which was of course the reason he had brought Mother along to "explain" it.

Well, there they were: he with egg on his chin, she in her bedroom slippers. "I overslept," she said unnecessarily.

"That's all right," I said.

"He's ever so slow and dopey," she added. "I don't suppose he'll get a scholarship, will he?"

Though he is only seven I was inclined in this case to concur.

In a more cheerful tone she continued: "We thought we'd let him learn the piano, then he could be a pianist. You know, on the halls. Or we thought he might be a commercial artist, he can draw good little pictures."

This recalled to me the words of a mother at another school where I had taught: "Sandra's no good at her school work, so her Dad and me are going to let her be a ballet dancer."

Isn't it odd, after seventy years or so of universal education in this country, that the notion should exist amongst masses of the educationally enfranchised that, unless you are "brainy", like a doctor or a teacher, educational and cultural standards are superfluous.

Can you be a pianist or a commercial artist or a ballet dancer without at the same time being literate? I have never known of a case. To bring the subject closer home, can you get much fun out of your school life if you are not literate?

Of all school subjects reading is perhaps the most important. I believe that whatever the method the children in a school should be able to read as soon and as well as possible.

This is not to suggest that the five-year-olds who are not ready to learn to read should be stampeded into doing so, but it does mean to encourage them from the word go to *want* to learn to read. A quantity of bright books set out so that the children have easy access to them, plenty of reading apparatus, and a teacher in a position to help a child as soon as he finds the desire for it are the three prerequisites for successful progress.

The last condition is, of course, the most important of them and, alas, the rarest to come by. A teacher with a class of fifty—a common number in city schools—will, even if she hears each child read for one minute per day, find that she has taken an hour out of every day and still not touched the problem of teaching her charges new sounds and words: a problem that can be neglected only at the child's cost. It therefore usually works out that with the best will in the world Primary school teachers cannot for the most part do as much as they would like.

It's another instance where the small school can steal an advantage. Not only are there fewer children; also they are never all at the same stage of development and need.

In reading each child in my school works at his and her own pace, and I try to hear every single one of them read every single day. Even the tiniest of them likes to feel that like the others he is "on a book" and, carefully avoiding placing a strain on them, I hear them read a few words from their book each day.

Five-year-old Willie—uncontrolled to a degree as to be officially considered slightly spastic—took this daily dose, to the general amazement, like the proverbial duck taking to water. He now reads so well that he has left seven-year-old Henry standing. You might not think this a miracle if you happened to know Henry; but one effect it has had is to jar Henry's pride. He is not as contented in his lethargy as he used to be.

In his aptitude Willie, it must be conceded, is an exception; but in his interest in reading he possesses only to a more pronounced degree what the others already share with him. A state of affairs like this can be established only, I think, where throughout their entire school life children are heard to read by a teacher every single day.

How is it fitted into *our* time-table?

There isn't a special time for it. (I exclude of course that regular period in the day when small numbers of children are surrounding my desk or the blackboard and learning from me new reading rules.)

My practice where reading is concerned is to listen to someone do it whenever I have a few minutes to spare. In the case of one or two of the older children I may hear them before school begins in the morning. "Head Boy" Eric seems to have now made it a matter of principle that he shall be the first to read to me before lessons begin. So we have five minutes together at this before the school is filled with arrivals.

Odd minutes are subsequently found to fit in the rest to this casual routine, and most of the children are at this stage quite keen to "have a turn".

I must stress again that I have been at this particular school for only a year so far, so that results in all spheres are in a tentative state where checking them is concerned.

There is one disadvantage from which my children here suffer: lack of incentive to read outside school. Some of them do not leave the village from one week's end to another, so that even the help in learning to read given to city children by the hoardings on the wall, the cinema advertisements and the shop windows are here lacking.

The nearest accessible public library is one and a half miles distant and functions only on Wednesdays between 6 and 7 p.m. (I hope soon to remedy this by arranging for a travelling library to visit us.)

Pondering on the kind of reading matter, if any, that my children encounter at home, I made some inquiries. I learned this:

> Five-year-old Willie's parents belong to a sixpence-a-week lending library at the newsagent's in our market town. At the other extreme lethargic little Henry's parents buy comics not only for Henry but for themselves. Father reads *Superman* and *Beano*, Mother reads *Girl*.
>
> Between these two poles come the other children's parents who take in newspapers, *Farmer's Weekly*, *Woman's Own*, and week-end papers like *Reveille* and *Week-end Mail*.
>
> The overwhelming part of winter evenings at home is spent watching television and listening to the wireless (Radio Luxembourg is the hot favourite); in summer it is working in the fields or the garden.

Asked what they themselves read at home, the children replied as follows:

> Ten-year-old Amy: *School Friend*, *Beano*, *Dandy*, *Woman's Own*. She possesses one book, *Playbox Annual*, which she has read twice.
>
> "Head Boy" Eric: *Topper*, *Playhour*. Was given "a book about trains" for Christmas, but found the print in it too difficult to read. Has no other books.
>
> Arthur, also nearly nine: *Topper*. Owns *Football Book*, *Chick's Own Annual*, *Rider of the West*, two of Enid Blyton's *Noddy* books and a book "about lorries". Can read them all "with a struggle".
>
> Mavis, eight: *Mickey Mouse Comic*, *Girl*. Owns a *Rupert* book and a book of poems that her mother bought for her. The poems are

read out to her by her brother. She has learned by heart a poem "about a fairy".

Peter, eight: *Junior Mirror* (today no longer published). Owns two *Noddy* books, *Schoolboys' Annual, Marvel Man, Cowboy Book, Roy Rogers' Knockout Book*. Can read them all.

Bernard, seven and a half: *Dandy, Beano, Topper*. Owns one book —*The Adventures of Robin Hood*—with pictures of Richard Todd as Robin Hood in the film of the book.

Beryl, seven and a half: a good reader, her sister attends the local Grammar School. She takes in no comics. Owns *Rupert* book, *Robin Annual, Little Grey Rabbit Goes to Sea, Schoolgirl's Annual, Knockout Fun Book, Enid Blyton's Holiday Book*, two *Noddy* books, *The Enchanted Wood, Bedtime Story Tales*.

Kate, eight: *Topper*. Looks at *Woman*. Owns one *Noddy* book, one *Rupert* book, *Holiday Book*.

Henry, seven: *TV Comic*. Glances at Father's *Beano* and *Superman* and Mother's *Girl*. Owns no books.

Susan, seven: *TV Comic, Topper, Beezer*. Owns two *Rupert* books, one *Noddy* book, *Cowboy Book*.

Elizabeth, six: No comics. Had a book at Christmas "about two cats".

Lily, five: No comics. Had a book at Christmas "about a dog".

Willie, five: *Robin, TV Comic, Beezer*. Owns two *Noddy* books, one train book.

Doris, five: *Chick's Own*. Has a book "about Jesus". Mother reads it to her.

Colin, five: *Playbox*. Owns a book about a dog and one about a train. Mother "too busy" to read them to him, but he looks at the pictures a lot.

There may be more books in the house than these children remember, but in no instance was an impression gained, or even scented, that there are numerous books in the home; and all but Willie maintained emphatically that their parents read no books.

Parents are here mentioned for a good reason. They are bound to influence the reading or non-reading habits of their children. In a home where television and the more unspeakable type of newspaper predominate there is not likely to co-exist with them sensible reading habits in the case of average or dull children.

It's obviously less strenuous to look at strip cartoons and at television. "Serious" reading is reserved for school time; and school time, as these children go up to the Junior department and need to do more and more reading, becomes less and less adequate for the task.

Our library consists of a quantity of outdated text books and dilapidated story books in the school cupboards. These books vary from a tattered *Alice in Wonderland* to a 1905 edition of *History Stepping-stones*, and some not very old paper-backed little books of adventure that are half cartoon, half writing. There are some books simpler in make-up than these for the youngest children. On all these borrowers, young and not so young, the librarian, "Head Boy" Eric, keeps a sharp, watchful tab. . . .

He feels, like many another man-in-charge, that nobody but himself can be trusted near the goods. He often complains to me: "They've left the books in a mess," though to my own casual eye the shelves always look excessively tidy.

The other morning, evidently succeeding an evening's brooding on the shortcomings of the Younger Generation, Eric turned up at school with an immense cardboard notice threaded with string, which he hung above the library shelves. In sinister block letters it read:

JUST YOU KEEP THESE SHELVES TIDY.
SIGNED, ERIC HUNT

Instead of grumbling at borrowers he now points to the notice and enjoins them: "Read that!"

Lethargic young Henry took him up on it and read out aloud: "Just you keep these sheep tiny," and, blinking in sleepy surprise at Eric, inquired: "What sheep?"

Here is a pointer to Henry's labours in reading. He would not think of saying to himself, "It's impossible that Eric should ask me to keep some sheep tiny," and then proceed to re-read the notice a little more alertly. No, for Henry words are capable of anything and so, apparently, is life. I don't think he would have been in the least put out had Eric in reply dragged out from the back of the shelves some tiny sheep and said: "These, of course."

Not that Eric is himself immune from occasional "howlers" in simple reading. Once at Morning Assembly, himself having chosen the hymn *We plough the fields and scatter*, he decided to help the smaller children by reading out to them part of each new verse before they were to sing it. Arriving at "He sends the snow in winter/The warmth to swell the grain", he rendered it: "He sends the snow in winter/The warmth to swell the grave."

His audience didn't blink an eye at such sentiments, and I couldn't forbear wondering whether the hymns our children sing so lustily are not in fact utterly incomprehensible to them. I recalled my own schooling and the lines from *Loving Shepherd of Thy Sheep*: "Where Thou leadest I would go/Walking in Thy steps below"—and passing a large part of my childhood in the belief that the Loving Shepherd, in this stanza, was leading us into some kind of cellar.

Though such misreadings are probably natural enough in childhood, it is self-evident that when allowing children to read to each other aloud particular care must be taken to ensure that the delivery is clearly enunciated, and as far as possible self-explanatory.

My older children love reading aloud to the younger ones, and the younger ones reciprocate by their love of listening. As it is so static an occupation I try to limit it to periods outside the school curriculum: wet playtimes, five-minute hiatuses near the end of the afternoon, or that short period between the time that the children have finished their dinner and the time when, after rest, they are ready to be let out to play.

Sometimes one Junior will read to all the Infants, sometimes one Junior has one Infant as audience. The stories are kept short and simple, so that the older child can read without hesitations, and consequently be free to emphasise enunciation and expression.

For all but the most advanced Juniors reading aloud is, I think, preferable to private reading. In a school like mine which is basically a kind of single large class one can, by making use of odd moments, give the Junior group a substantial quantity of this very useful practice.

On more formal occasions I try to give even the smaller children a chance to "shine" in public.

As stated, we have short Bible readings at some of the Morning Assemblies. We have a Poetry Reading group once a week, when the Juniors prepare to read aloud poems of their own choosing. To the smaller children is granted an opportunity to read aloud any page in their reading books that they can read particularly well. Mild incentive though this is, it is greatly prized by the five- and six-year-olds who find even the meanest of public appearances awesome.

The Infants feel even more honoured if a story they have written or an extract from their diary is considered worthy of interesting the others when read out to them. Often what they have written is odd enough to amuse the Juniors as well as give them, on hearing it, a satisfying feeling of their own grown-upness.

Six-year-old Elizabeth read out what she had written about the Rector:

> He has a church, and he lives with his dogs. He wears striped trousers and a top hat. I go to his church and sing the hymns.

Smiles verge on the Juniors' faces as they listen to this unusual pen-portrait. When I suggested to them: "What about you trying your hand at describing the Rector?" they set to it with a competitive vigour and zeal.

Whatever schemes are evolved for furthering the cause of reading, a fine incentive, undoubtedly, is the possession of a wide assortment of attractive books. Building up such an assortment is not, unhappily, an inexpensive task. Having been recently given a twenty-pound grant we are luckily here in the position of owning an abundance of books not yet exhaustively read. To these, too, the children have free access at all times, and they have contributed almost as much as any other single factor to the encouragement to read.

The children advise each other on what each thinks are the best books and pore over them with a diligence that would send a glow of self-satisfaction over the authors of them were they privileged to witness the spectacle.

Here too personality obtrudes itself.

Ten-year-old Amy will absorbedly burrow her way through the book she has chosen and never through shyness volunteer to ask me the meaning or the correct pronunciation of a word that confounds her. Nearly-nine-year-old Arthur makes a conspicuous song and dance about any book he views as "smashing", but if left alone he skips through each of them with lightning speed, and is permanently at the cupboard seeking a new one and offering unsolicited literary opinions about what he has read to whoever he finds there. Susan, aged seven, who is at the stage of reading with confidence, is unable to contain her pride at this, and reads her book aloud to the other children at her table, substituting, for the words she doesn't know, invented ones of her own that seem to bridge the gap.

And Henry? Henry opens his book, then forgets about it and sits gazing before him into space, stifling an occasional yawn, until it is time for the books to be put away. . . .

THE WORLD AROUND US

FOR my children the village is their world. There are those who have been as far as some seaside or other—for holidays-by-the-sea is more of an urban than a rural custom—and those, often the same ones, who have visited the zoo in some large city.

Very nearly all of them have seen one Christmas pantomime, and the same percentage have at least one relation who lives elsewhere than in the village.

This about completes their contact with the "big" world.

One other "experience" may perhaps be mentioned in this connection: on one or two occasions in the year the village is invaded by two dilapidated Indians wearing turbans and carrying suit-cases bulging with blouses and nylon stockings. Their singular enunciation of our mother tongue comes over to us in a high-pitched tone that intrigues my children. I was first made aware of these pedlars by seven-year-old Bernard dashing back in to school from a visit to the W.C. with the alarming announcement:

"There's two Blackies come in the street!"

While I was still debating with myself where to begin in decoding this message Eric volunteered: "It's not Blackies. I know what he means."

"Good," I said with relief.

Eric continued: "They comes every year. They sells clothes."

Unenlightened, still, I inquired: "Who do?"

Eric seemed to have shot his bolt. He felt in his ignorance—I imagine—that anything further he might say on the subject could, as the police so nastily put it, be used against him.

Pitying his dilemma, I turned to ten-year-old Amy for succour; but she was wearing what I always think of as her Mona Lisa smile, an expression that invariably accompanies her most obdurate silences.

Fortunately there is one person in the class whom nothing daunts: nearly-nine-year-old Arthur. He is prepared to have an explanation or to provide one without notice for any phenomenon you care to name. He is the kind of boy who, as an adult, you will often find holding the collective attention of the public bar or, higher up in the social scale, chairing a Brains Trust on the B.B.C.

On the subject of "the Blackies" he gave spluttering utterance to these wise words:

"They don't live in this country. They wear cloth things on their 'eads."

Eight-year-old Peter, who had recently been reading *Ali Baba*, came to my rescue and impressed us all by interpolating:

"Turbans!"

Light mercifully dawned on me. "Indians, are they?" I said.

"Of course!" said Eric, in a tone that I think was meant to

persuade me that he had known all along and had merely been testing *my* knowledge.

Like their sense of place, as here shown, their sense of time is equally confused.

Here is something of an encounter between eight-year-old Mavis and seven-and-a-half-year-old Beryl. Beryl can read well, but is still rather babyish in other ways; whereas Mavis has a five-and-a-half-year-old reading age but is a big, physically mature sort of girl and older than Beryl.

Beryl had brought to school a pink fan with which she intended to play in the school's Wendy House one afternoon, and she showed it to Mavis, explaining: "It's our Mum's."

Mavis, who shares with Eric a weakness for perpetually putting other people "right", responded: "They only has those in olden days."

"They don't," Beryl said. "Our Mum took it to the dance when she used to go."

"Well, she couldn't," said Mavis. "She's never lived in the olden days, has she?"

"She might have," Beryl said defensively.

This gave Mavis a laugh. "Lived in the olden days? She'd be dead now!" She inquired, blandly: "Is she dead?"

"Of course not," Beryl said weakly.

"Well, then, there you are!" concluded Mavis.

And that was—definitely—that. . . .

I am hoping that these two conversation-pieces indicate the shortcomings inherent in teaching history and geography to children in the form of isolated events. It results in the peoples of other lands being seen as oddities, and in ages other than our own being ringed round in the mind as islands of time in human history and cut off from the rest of it.

We as adults know that no place or time is a static entity, that history and geography are fluid processes, that the present could not be what it is without the past, and that without the merging of these two elements the future could not be born.

To get this basic notion across to Junior children is difficult but not, to my mind, impossible. If not done we not only cut them off from a rightful heritage of knowledge but implicitly present them with a world denuded of moral law and arbitrary to the last degree in its natural functionings.

In our school there is a set of reasonably new books labelled "geography". They are attractively produced, and they are devoted to telling the story of child-life in other lands. A worthy aim at first glance. At a second glance its inadequacies are glaring: its basic reference is English childhood which it glorifies as a kind of "norm", so that childhood in other lands become grotesque deviations from it instead of existing nobly in their own right. French children are depicted exclusively in wooden sabots, German children in embroidered braces and eternally munching sausage, Chinese in pigtails and armed with chopsticks, Red Indians in wigwams and babies strapped to their backs; and by the time we get to the section devoted to pygmies and bushmen authorship has run riot.

To try at the same time to teach children that in the eyes of God all men are brothers or, in the words of St. Paul, that we are members one of another, is to add not enlightenment but confusion.

The child's notion of the world outside the boundaries of its everyday life teems, I think we would all agree, with phantom mystery and magic. To endorse this notion by our teachings is to build a high, dark wall round it, whereas our real duty surely lies in extending the child's knowledge of the wider world at the expense of his hobgoblin version of it, so that children like seven-year-old Bernard do not grow up with the fixed idea that the part of the universe which he occupies is God-ordained and the rest inhabited by "Blackies" and such-like.

In combating the traditional methods in my own school in teaching I made a start with geography.

Just after the late war I visited the famous Pestalozzi Community in Switzerland. I have been using this experience as my springboard for the plunge into geography. First I told the story of my visit: why I went, how I got there, what I found when I arrived.

With that spontaneous sympathy natural to children they responded instantly to an account describing orphans being brought together under the care of kindly adults. The idea of a "village of children" had an appeal they could not resist. The possibilities in such a scheme of teaching geography multiply at the pace that enthusiasm enlarges. There is no other way of teaching them geography at present that competes in scope or liveliness.

Not least in importance among the results of this method is that children in other lands emerge as real: with names, personal histories, birthdays. Their "national" characteristics do not as a consequence provoke laughter or an incredulous gape, but are seen, as they should indeed be seen, as colourful constituents in the contemporary racial pattern.

We possess photographs of various houses in the "village" where these orphans live and photographs exhibiting them at their many occupations. Photographs always show a community at its best.

I think we all recognise security as being at the heart of a child's needs, and it must have been one of the reasons why Pestalozzi so gripped the imagination of my children. Mavis asked me one day: "If you've got no Mum and Dad in this country what do they do with you?"

Eric told her: "You goes to an orphanage."

As their notion of an orphanage was no less wildly vague than their notion of what two Indian pedlars were doing in invading the village with suit-cases and turbans, I told them a little of what I thought I knew about the subject.

Seven-year-old Beryl said: "I should go to live at our Gran's!"

Eric, impatient with Inferior Minds, ejaculated: "*She's* telling us where you goes if you *hasn't* got a Gran."

(For some reason that he will probably carry with him undivulged to the grave he always refers to me as "she".)

For weeks the children wanted nothing so much as to listen to whatever I could tell them about this remarkable village in Switzerland, and they were particularly delighted at Christmas when its reality was established for them beyond doubt by my presenting each of them with a handkerchief manufactured in Pestalozzi and sold internationally as part of a fund-raising scheme.

The next step was my decision that the time had arrived for my Juniors to contribute to these lessons. Each week we selected a child from our Pestalozzi dossier and tried to discover all we could about him as a human being. I fashioned a large map with Pestalozzi marked clearly and conspicuously on it, and by means of the coloured bands in use by the children we were able to identify all the countries—including England—from which children had travelled to live in Pestalozzi.

Our first entry is FRANCE. It is typical of the method and perhaps worthy of elaboration. We chose an imaginary boy called Pierre, who is supposed to have come to Pestalozzi from Paris, and we tried to build up him and his background.

In the process we learned two French songs that Pierre might be reasonably thought to know: *Au clair de la lune* and *Frère Jacques*. Five-year-old Willie's father has two French coins. I own a couple of French story-books. Eight-year-old Peter found a book at home with a picture of the French tricolour in it. He was not permitted to bring the book to school, but he copied out the flag for us with meticulous care. We stuck it in our Class Book. Mavis brought us a picture postcard of the Eiffel Tower that her sister's "young man" sent her from there when serving overseas in the late war.

Everyone had a try at painting their version of Pierre (sabots barred!) based on photographs of the French boys in Pestalozzi. Then they described his habits: what kind of food he would prefer, the games he was likely to play.

The writing was, of course, limited to Juniors who could draw for inspiration upon simple books of reference that I borrowed for them from libraries.

In work of this kind details about children of various countries can be elaborated to eventually include the general characteristics of the country concerned, touching for instance upon the distance and the kind of journey you would have to make from it to Pestalozzi.

A by-product of all this is the growth among my children of an interest in organisations other than the Pestalozzi one that specialise in the care of the many young in today's world who are without homes or family. Quite a quantity of discarded clothing was collected for them at Christmas by my children who, in the process, discovered an agreeable sense of their own good fortune in having homes that others of their kind lacked.

When as a small girl I refused to eat crusts my mother would say: "Plenty of children would be glad to have them."

I never took this phrase as anything but a fanciful adult threat of the usual overdone kind, and I find it an odd experience to over-hear Mavis telling young Willie at dinner: "Don't you waste that potato! If you was like them children without enough food to eat you'd be glad of it."

Willie, for whom Mavis's strictures are too subtle (not to say tiresome!), replies: "I'm full," which leads Mavis to deflect her impassioned appeal to the bystanders: " '*E throws away good food when other children is hungry!*"

It is on this particular basis of caring-for-others that our nature study, too, is pursued: looking after the fish kept in school, the bird table in the playground, visits to local farms to inspect animals and their conditions, visits to Peter's father who owns an aviary, care of Mrs. Duckworth's cat who spends the day in school, and of course the school garden.

The children write a good deal about these activities and learn in the process, I believe, a good deal about them.

It was a surprise to me when I first came to the country to find how little natural history country children know. Beyond the most common flowers and birds the distinctions between various forms of life around them are unknown to the children I have taught. I am no great shakes as a botanist, but I have found that explorations of the countryside with books of reference, and the means to bring back whatever treasures are encountered there, can be quite profitable. We have got to the stage of regularly sending packets of wild flowers and leaves we have picked up on these walks to some school in the centre of an industrial city where the phenomena are unknown.

This, too, helps to clear from my children's minds the hitherto fixed notion that they constitute some kind of isolated and exclusive community; and in the exercise of the fraternal practice itself the older children have learned how to pack carefully flowers that are intended to reach a destination uncrushed. The cost of it is shared by us all.

To link the study of history with everyday life was, I found, more of a "poser"; but I luckily picked up a useful hint in the report of a recent women's institute conference.

A number of institutes had compiled a history of their own village from as far back as the records could take them until the present day. On reading the results it seemed to me an approach to history worth emulating, with the possibility thrown in of linking the findings with local topography.

The book we are making, christened by the resourceful Eric "Everything about our Village", is by no means on the point of completion, but there are discoveries so far made that leave even Mrs. Duckworth incredulous.

An old man, much older than she, has been unearthed, as it were, who remembers having to haul up the flag on the village green when the squire was in residence, and to lower it to half-mast when the squire was away in London hazarding life and limb to bring back his lady silks and satins from the shops. There is also among the records a faded broadsheet left as a family heirloom by the grandfather of an old lady at present alive in the village in which he describes the experience of being held up by a highwayman and the man's eventual capture.

Highwaymen—is it needless to add?—were for some time after this the main source of playground games in school. The only drawback to its successful deployment as such was everyone's disinclination to accept any other role but that of the highwayman. I heard Eric appeal: "Listen, you kids, you can't all be highwaymen. There's got to be somebody to hold up. You has to have people in the coach coming along the road," but the general response to this reasoning was that someone other than the recruit appealed to should play the necessary part of "the people". It needed all Eric's persuasion—as well as some ambiguous threats of coercion—to get his hearers into an imaginary coach and have the part of the highwayman left in the hands of the only person qualified to do it justice: himself, naturally.

Apart from written records and personal reminiscences to help us in our task there is the "living history" of our attractive Norman church partly renovated in the sixteenth century and again in the nineteenth. Standing there to be inspected, examined and discussed at will, it lends itself admirably as an aid to tracing local history back to its early beginnings.

The children are at present working on a model of the village as it most probably looked about one hundred years back, at a time when an ancestor of one of our school managers habitually gave twenty pounds per year to be distributed on St. Thomas's Day "among the needy poor of this Parish". The tradition is continued today, no longer in the form of meat and bread but in gift vouchers presented to old-age pensioners who may translate them into what they will at the nearest shop.

Six-and-a-half-year-old Edith painted the picture of an old man on St. Thomas's Day bringing home a large brown cottage loaf and a string of sausages as his share of the gift. His old wife was portrayed waiting for him at their cottage door and beneath Edith had written:

> She's seeing he brings them straight home and don't eat them on the way. He's a naughty old man.

Being as it may on this light-hearted level, the history and geography my children study are nevertheless matters in which they are actively immersed, and who knows what else they may be learning in the process! One thing I do hope they are learning in it: that they are not part of some little island of space or time but components of a universe that stretches around, behind and—most seductively of all—before them.

ART AND CRAFT

AS a teacher the first school caretaker I ever encountered was a certain Mr. Watkins.

The school it was his duty to keep clean for us was ancient and large, and—as Mr. Watkins saw it—packed with messy children and a careless staff. In his embittered opinion scraps of paper were each day littered about the premises solely for the vindictive purpose of having him pick them up. I don't know if he was a subscriber to that immortal schoolboys' periodical, *The Magnet*, but if he was I imagine he must have been in whole-hearted sympathy with "Gosling", the porter of Greyfriars School, who never referred to the scholars as anything but "them little varmints".

Our Mrs. Duckworth would be genuinely shocked at such a sentiment, but she nevertheless shares Mr. Watkins's conviction

75

that a teacher's primary duty is to leave the school building as tidy as she finds it.

It's for this reason that Mrs. Duckworth's preference in educational methods, like so many caretakers', is the sit-still-and-write-in-your-copy-book type so widely practised in her own infancy. It means less work for the caretaker after school, whereas the freer, contemporary methods of education mean more work for the caretaker after school.

In her determination not to be disillusioned about me she prefers to believe that in the practice of these freer, untidy methods I am more sinned against than sinning in that I am a victim of the passion for experiment on the part of school inspectors. She refuses to believe—dear, loyal soul!—that left alone I would so lack a sense of responsibility as to introduce into the classroom a giant bin of clay, saws, planks of wood, bowls of water, trays of sand and all the other nightmarish paraphernalia of a caretaker's life.

It's not her custom to voice her horror; but there was one occasion when a visiting inspector thought it might be interesting to combine clay- and water-play. "Small children do love being messy," was his charitable pretext for the operation.

It might have turned out "interesting"—without being disastrous at the same time—had five-year-old, near-spastic Willie taken the afternoon off; but no, not only was Willie very much present, he put everything he had into making it a red-letter day for himself by hurling lumps of clay into a bowl of water until the inspector called a halt. I think Willie came away from school that day with a very high opinion of inspectors; but it was left to me to make peace with Mrs. Duckworth when she came to tidy up after school.

She shook her head as she surveyed the mess on the floor, commenting bravely: "Never mind, it doesn't happen very often. You can't help accidents, can you?"

I couldn't after that bring myself to tell her it was no accident but an intentional part of Willie's "creative development". She might have had a fit. Certainly the least that would have happened would have been the sound of the rafters ringing out the echo of Mrs. Duckworth's favourite comment: "I'm sure I don't know what the world's coming to and that's a fact."

I just let it go. It's not my business to "educate" Mrs. Duckworth, and she wouldn't thank me for it if I tried.

She by no means stands alone in regarding modern methods in education with a distrustful eye and inspectors as licensed clowns. When the County Library sent me a batch of children's books the librarian who brought them in a travelling van explained the simple procedure involved in loaning them out, and added: "Some inspectors have been urging headmistresses to let the children do the filing themselves, and it's resulted in some frightful muddles for *us*. It should be done by an adult, you see. It was just never meant as an *activity*"—yes, she emphasised the last word. She evidently saw "activity" as a kind of free-for-all where chaos is, paradoxically, the order of the day.

I uttered not a word in contradiction of this attitude; I merely made a mental resolve to let ten-year-old Amy try her hand at it with me keeping an eye on the proceedings.

As the borrowers of these books consist of only eight Junior children Amy has no bother in the "filing". It's just the kind of thing she likes to do: it involves a scanty amount of conversation and no limelight, and yet is pleasingly a position of trust and responsibility.

Being, as far as size goes, a kind of cat among the pigeons at school, Amy relishes those activities that she can perform alone or with no more than the aid of eight-year-old, stolid Mavis— with whom, incidentally, she seems to share a kind of deep, inarticulate friendship. At least I *thought* it was inarticulate until the day I asked Mavis: "Is Amy as quiet with you as she is with me?" and got the thought-provoking reply: "Oh, no, she talks all the time."

Well, wherever it is that "she talks all the time" it isn't in school. Even in the afternoon, when bustle and chatter seethe around her, she will sit quietly and sew, embroider, weave, knit or read. She is a steady worker and her achievements are of the cumulative sort. In the course of two terms she knitted for herself a matching scarf, hat, pair of mittens. A tray cloth was another thing she designed and embroidered. She also drew, and stitched in tapestry wool, a picture of a bitch and its puppy on a linen background. Another thing she did was to back a picture with yellow cardboard so that it could be hung on the wall. In co-operation with Mavis she wove a table-centre and four table-mats for use in the Wendy House. She is not markedly creative and the work she does is scarcely ever original or even unexpected, but it is a fact that whatever she begins is worked at solidly until it is done.

Her opposite in this respect is nearly-nine-year-old, ebullient young Arthur. I can't think of a thing in the world that Arthur would not volunteer to undertake with the wildest enthusiasm at the least encouragement; and, conversely, there is nothing in the world in the way of tasks that I can imagine him completing. Arthur, I fear, may develop into one of those engaging but sometimes tiresome characters you meet in public places who know—and insist on telling—how the country could be run more efficiently than the current Prime Minister is doing it if the speaker's advice were taken and followed. It is fascinating to speculate that somewhere in the world are young people who will one day be adults listening with goggle-eyed respect to Arthur's pronouncements; and somewhere else other children, perhaps less patient, who will one day as adults be dashing out of their arm-chairs to leave a room whenever they hear Arthur's voice approaching it.

He is the dilettante *par excellence*, the as-it-were artistic butterfly —if Arthur and his clumping great boots can surmount the strain of such a vision—flitting from experiment to experiment with nothing to show for an afternoon's work in school except a certain weariness in the legs.

Luckily, Amy and Arthur are both extreme types of children when it comes to learning-through-doing; the majority take an almost exquisite delight in the act of making or creating.

When it comes to art and craft the teacher has to be careful to see that, though she may help and guide, she does not get to the point of actually showing her charges what to do.

Children's efforts in the unravelling of the potentialities of any new medium can seem very crude by adult standards, and we have to ensure that we don't get impatient with them. When five-year-old Colin first attended school he did his painting on a large sheet of previously whitewashed newspaper with the wrong end of the brush, oblivious of the far more effective way of doing it.

There was no other child near him, so he was left to find out the delightful truth for himself. I happened to have my eye on him when this revelation occurred. He examined the brush, and then abruptly turned it the other way and dipped the bristles instead of the handle in the paint. When the superior results appeared on the paper a slow smile spread across his face as though he were thinking: "What a clever fellow you are, Colin! Making a discovery like that on your first day at school!"

I was glad I hadn't succumbed earlier to the temptation to show him how . . . I wonder how often we rob children in school and in the home of the joys of discovery?

Children do, of course, come to one of their own accord to ask: "How do you do this?" or "What shall I paint now?" or "What can I make?" and though help in such an instance has to be granted it can certainly be cut down to a minimum in a school where art and craft are an organic part of the curriculum, and not looked upon as merely "handwork lessons".

It's pleasant from time to time to show children how to make a paper kite, or a necklace from paper beads, or a tiny house out of empty match-boxes, but lessons of this sort should be the exception rather than the rule. Art and craft can bestow so satisfying an experience and such stimulus on the creative instinct that it would be a great pity from every point of view to make some rigid decision beforehand on how a lesson shall progress or even on how long it shall last.

In a small school like mine, where a time-table can be an extremely fluid arrangement, periods of work can spill over into each other without causing inconvenience, and different children can be doing different things from one another at the same time. Noise, remember, is disturbing to the teacher rather than to the children. A boy like eight-year-old Peter can absorb himself in reading *The Wind in the Willows* without seemingly being aware that some yards away Bernard and Arthur are laughing themselves silly over a game of *Snakes and Ladders*. My children mostly come from homes where the wireless and television are kept running like a dripping tap, and whoever in the family wants to do anything that needs concentration has to learn immunity from these household pests. I think most children get the knack of it soon.

I do, all the same, try to separate the noisy activities from the other sort. Woodwork, for instance, is usually relegated to the cloakroom. When the weather permits I send the youngest children to play with their pull-along toys in the playground. Under similar conditions they will take their giant building bricks out there. There is a great supply of rush mats and the more worn of these are handy for sitting on in the playground. The playground, not having to be shared with other classes as in a city school, is a kind of open-air room that we can fall back on in emergency.

Art and craft is divided into three sections in my school: there is individual work, there is work done in small groups co-operating spontaneously, and there is the big, organised, communal effort where everyone helps. This last is often the most dramatic in execution and the most gratifying when accomplished.

By these means we have in the past year made two large paper-mosaic murals: a cause of perpetual pride to its authors. One of these murals, six feet square, was made for Christmas and depicts the Nativity. The background is of black paper and the human figures and animals from material comprising shiny toffee wrappings, crinkly cracker paper, silver paper, coloured snippets from innumerable women's periodicals and scraps of wool.

Even Willie, whose muscular control is poor, managed to contribute some little silver stars for the sky and helped with the wild flowers that it was conjectured might have been growing outside the stable.

The second mural, more ambitious in that it incorporates other materials additional to coloured paper, is entitled "Wash Day", and depicts Mother washing, and clothes blowing on the line. Inspired by Bernard, who produced a piece of shirt-tail from which to make a miniature shirt to hang on the line, the other children decided to have all the clothes that were to hang on the line of the correct material.

This naturally led them on to *appliqué* work. The smaller children made cardboard dolls which they dressed in a variety of scraps of material: velvet, cotton, ribbons, printed linens. These materials were sometimes pasted on, sometimes affixed with a stitch or two. They have since been used also as extra "babies" in games of Mothers-and-Fathers in the Wendy House.

"Head Boy" Eric revealed an unexpected talent for sewing and stitched together most attractively a blackbird eating berries from a hawthorn bush. (It was a copy of a picture originally painted by Peter which hangs on the wall.) It got itself some unusual attention because of the almost repulsive vitality of the blackbird who quite dwarfs the bush. Eric framed the result in manilla paper and hung it on the wall beside its hand-painted replica, and the children were intrigued to see how different the outcome can be when a theme is treated in two dissimilar media.

As for the second division in the art-and-craft curriculum, work achieved by the co-operation of small groups of children most often arises initially from their play or from the stimulation received as the result of the telling of some story.

For instance, the Wendy House has launched many an idea: one started a group of girls making tiny sausages out of silk stockings, "so as I can give the babies", as Mavis explained it, "a good breakfast". Another was an experiment in fabric printing by Amy and Eric for the curtains of the Wendy House. Another occurred when our village storekeeper, Mr. Homans, handed lethargic little Henry an orange box. Though Henry usually exhausts his physical resources bringing just himself to school he freely took on the burden on this occasion of bringing the orange box with him. The first thing that happened was a discussion on what to do with it. Arthur typically suggested a jet aeroplane or a tractor, for in theory Arthur (like the late Henry Ford) will have no truck with anything petty or less than sensational. His inspired suggestion met from Eric the dampening response: "We wants proper ideas. You always have silly ones."

The "proper" idea eventually took shape in the making of a truck. Peter brought to school four old pram wheels, Henry's orange box was sandpapered and painted, two holes were drilled in front for a rope to be threaded through; and Henry was allowed pride of place at the helm on account of its being his orange box. Eric sat behind him. The rest of the boys pulled them both along. It has since proved itself a useful stand-by in plays.

Junior children with their marked energy and enthusiasm enjoy "big" projects of this nature, and it is particularly profitable for them to undertake the making of something that cannot be completed in a day, and for which they need to find additional materials—like Peter's four old pram wheels for the "truck"—as well as a sustained keenness.

In the cause of these projects my children have become expert scavengers. Into a large "oddments" box we keep in the classroom goes anything they find that might be useful, from lengths of string to disused toilet rolls. Parents' help has been enlisted in this cause, and fathers will often send along bits of wood, pieces of wire netting, and even an occasional paint-pot with a residue of "real" paint at the bottom.

Mothers can usually find scraps of wool and materials like it, for which with us there is always a shortage; this is a perennial difficulty attending free activity in art and craft. I do a good deal of begging from local factories and shops, and in one way and another we somehow manage, but nevertheless it is what is known as a hand-to-mouth existence.

An advantage here in the country with work of this sort is that sheep's wool can be collected in surprising quantities from hedgerows and fences, for it has been a woollen centre since before Chaucer's time, and indeed in the fifteenth century "Cotswold wool was considered the best in England and therefore in Europe",[1] although, of course, it no longer enjoys this hegemony.

Incomparably greater pleasure can be derived from weaving with this material collected, prepared and dyed by the children themselves—than with shop wool. Until they started doing this my children, I suspect, were in a position similar to the legendary city boy who believed that milk comes from bottles and not from cows. It's true that they had often seen sheep, but oddly had never connected their dirty, shaggy coats with the neat and gleaming hanks of wool they normally saw in use at home.

Infant and Junior handicrafts should, I feel, be adding to the child's accumulating knowledge of the world, especially in the province of learning where it is constantly asked: How is it made? How does it work?

More important still, the practice of them can lay the foundation of that all too rare and oft-debated quality: good taste. The child who has fired and painted his own pottery, experimented with pattern and design, acquired familiarity with the fundamentals of bookbinding and the superiority of appeal in attractive lettering, played with colour and texture in the making and dressing of puppets—such a child stands a better chance than an untutored one of not being perpetually taken in by the multitude of manufactured products infesting the world around him irrespective of their disparate worth. And who knows? He may even get as far as growing into the kind of adult who will take a look at some mass-produced article and think: "I could do better than this, myself"—and sit down and do it.

[1] G. M. Trevelyan's *English Social History*, page 86

I saw Esau kissing Kate.
The fact is we all three saw;
For I saw him
And he saw me
And she saw I saw Esau.

THE RING OF WORDS

IVES there the child who will not joyfully learn and chant such jingles as fast as his teacher cares to provide them? I doubt it.

Ah—we think—if only they would be as enthusiastic about *all* poetry. . . .

It's my belief that if children are indifferent to the poems we provide for them there is something wrong with the poems or the manner in which they are served up. They may be bad poems. There are multitudes of them in school anthologies: poems around synthetic emotions like the there-are-fairies-at-the-bottom-of-our-garden type; poems that get into anthologies solely because they rhyme as, for example, *I think mice/Are rather nice*; poems based on baby talk and thereby thought "suitable for the young" as, for example, *I had nuffink/No, I didn't have nuffink—*

the type of poem that particularly leaves children bewildered that Teacher, who is usually so fussy about correct speech, should be opting for such heresies as *No, I didn't have nuffink*.[1]

Also there are poems that are perfectly good as poems, but not particularly suited to the age-group or tastes of the children we happen to be teaching. I recall myself at the age of nine, when "heavy" poetry was still in fashion, chanting with total incomprehension the details of *How they brought the Good News from Ghent to Aix*, and its brother-in-ambiguity, "Abou Ben Adhem and the Angel".

I am not claiming that I was any the worse for learning these poems, but that they had fired me and the rest of the class with a passion for poetry—which they ought to have done—is a claim that would be even more preposterous were I to make it.

Two conditions are absolutely vital if poetry is to obtain a grip on the young mind: the poems offered must be good, "honest" poems and they must be of a kind to appeal to their audience. Perhaps there is a third condition that should scarcely need stressing: the poem should not be murdered in delivery. By this I mean that children should not be ordered to chant a poem collectively, or even singly, to ensure that they have learned it. It may make a pretty impression on some old-fashioned inspector, but as a method of inculcating in the young a love of poetry it is a waste of energy in all parties involved.

I have never forgotten a remark made to me by the English master when I was at my grammar school, after hearing me mouth in an insipid, sing-song fashion Keats's poem, *Meg Merrilies*, that I had learned by heart for the delectation of my admiring friends. "Don't spoil the poem," he said. "It doesn't belong to you."

What he would have thought of a teacher I happen to know who blithely changes the words in any poem that she thinks "difficult" for her class, I prefer not to think about!

Children will often, of course, do this; but unconsciously. Five-year-old Lily in my school happily recites: "Little Miss Muffet/ Sat on a tuffet/Eating her curls away," and further up the age-scale

[1] These examples are taken from well-known contemporary books for children

the irrepressively ebullient Arthur renders the words *Teach us delight in simple things*: "Teachers delight in simple things."

Eight-year-old Peter, our best reader, gets *his* unusual "effects" in spelling. It has often reminded me of Winnie the Pooh's verdict on his own spelling: "It's good spelling but it Wobbles." In Peter's story of the Good Samaritan appears the following sentence: "The Good Samaritan came by, took pity on him and wrapped him in a cloak," which reads: "The Good Samaritan came by, took pity on him and raped him in a cloak."

My children possess so impoverished a vocabulary, and so lamely is it used, that they have, I think, a very special need for poetry and literature.

Poetry readings I make as informal as possible, and on each occasion I try to include as wide a variety of poems I can find so as to have something that appeals to everybody.

For these readings Juniors and Infants collect together in a single group. The Juniors, who are by city standards "unsophisticated", are able to listen to, and enjoy endlessly, the nursery rhymes and simple verses that the Infants like best.

I believe the Juniors benefit from this. Most children have far too sparse and conventional a repertoire of nursery rhymes and jingles which, when the children reach Junior school, tend to be dropped altogether. Yet is there not immense and permanent beauty and joy to be derived from such rhymes as:

> *The hart he loves the high wood,*
> *The hare she loves the hill;*
> *The knight he loves his bright sword,*
> *The lady loves her will.*[1]
>
> or:
>
> *The herring loves the merry moonlight,*
> *The mackerel loves the wind;*
> *But the oyster loves the dredging song,*
> *For she comes of a gentle kind.*[2]

When I recited this last jingle to the children eight-year-old Mavis, who in spite of her semi-illiteracy has an ear for words,

[1] Anonymous   [2] Anonymous

said: "Fancy calling the moonlight merry! I thought merry is when you laughs."

Six-and-a-half-year-old Edith informed her (and us): "Well, I've seen the man in the moon and he looks as if he's laughing."

Isn't it this spontaneous kind of interest in the words of a poem that we teachers so often find so difficult to generate?

When it does happen I think we are justified in believing that we have chosen the right poem for our group.

An additional reward for providing the right poem is that the children want to hear it again and again, so that finally it is learned without any strenuously conscious effort on anyone's part.

Children having as little to do with the English language as mine in their daily life obviously, it seems to me, ought to learn as much poetry as they can imbibe. To have embedded in their minds even such simple phrases as "bright swords", "merry moonlight" and "high wood" can be infinitely to their enrichment. Poverty of expression on the child's part can inject a vitiating element in its relations with a teacher. Yet what child— excluding the one with a most unusual mind or home—will have stored up in its head exciting and unconventional phrases unless the desire to learn the poems from whence these came is a consequence of the child's will rather than that of the teacher's?

I know dozens of lovely little poems that I would like my children to learn, but they are not likely to learn them simply because I like them. How then is one to get the children to like them?

A first condition is, of course, that I myself shall like the poems I am offering them. Do teachers invariably like the poems they choose to read to their class?

My own likes vary from inconsequential limericks such as the anonymous:

> There was a young man of Bengal
> Who went to a fancy-dress ball.
> He went just for fun,
> Dressed up as a bun,
> And a dog ate him up in the hall.

to this by John Fletcher (1579–1625):

> *Do not fear to put thy feet*
> *Naked in the River sweet;*
> *Think not Leach, nor Newt or Toad*
> *Will bite thy foot, when thou hast troad;*
> *Nor let the water rising high,*
> *As thou wad'st in, make thee crie*
> *And sob, but ever live with me,*
> *And not a wave shall trouble thee.*[1]

Never do I tell the children: "Today we will learn this poem. Say it a line at a time after me."

I think it far better for me to read the poem frequently, encouraging the children to join in as they choose. In this way each child can pick up bits of the poem that he particularly likes, or even the whole poem (I've no objection!). Lines or verses that have been learned as a result of one falling in love with them are rarely—we would surely all agree—forgotten.

Another advantage in the method of not pegging away to the bitter end of a single poem is that it leaves time for much more poetry—as well a keener sense of freedom and enjoyment in the reading of it than there would be on the dreary lines of the this-must-be-learned school of thought.

While poetry reading for Infants in my school consists exclusively of listening to poetry being recited and, if they choose, reciting it themselves, for the Juniors there are variations on this theme. One is that each takes his turn once a month in collecting a group of poems from books of poetry provided by me, copies out those he likes, illustrates them and on occasion reads them out aloud. Every-child-his-own-editor is the idea.

For this purpose I buy as many single books of good poems and rhymes as I can find and my allowance permits, so that there is now a whole shelf full of poetry books to which the children, provided their hands are clean, have ready access.

Last term ten-year-old Amy's anthology—"poetry book", we

[1] From *The Faithful Shepherdess*, Act III, Scene 1

call it—based on a notion inspired initially by a reading of T. S. Eliot's *Old Possum's Book of Practical Cats*, concerned itself with the theme of birds. It included:

The Blackbird—Humbert Wolfe
The Linnet Has Her Song—J. Shercliff
The Dove Says Coo—Anon.
The Birds—Hilaire Belloc
A Song—Shelley

Also from the *Observer Book of British Birds* she painstakingly illustrated pictures of birds that took her fancy. Although the total result lacked—not surprisingly—the gaiety of the Eliot book, it was nevertheless a genuine labour of love. That is the best, and a good best it is, that one can say for it.

Making up one's *own* poems is a far more onerous business where my children are concerned. At present the younger—less inhibited!—children seem to do better at it than the older ones. Lethargic little Henry surprisingly romped home with a winner in:

I have a dog,
It is named Risky.
I tickles his tummy
And it makes him frisky.

"Head Boy" Eric threw in gratis the anti-climactic couplet:

I gives him beer
And it makes him tipsy.

Emotion is a thing Henry is not extravagantly given to— his meagre fund of energy presumably forbids it—but this *mot juste* of Eric's had him, as the saying goes, rolling in the aisles.

For him, as for the others, vistas undreamed of had been opened up by the possibilities in the power of rhyme.

Grasping at the moment of illumination I suggested: "Let's make up rhymes about each other."

Seven-and-a-half-year-old Beryl wrote:

> *My friend Kate*
> *Is never late.*
> *She comes to school early*
> *And is always before me.*
> *Every day*
> *We play.*
> *We only plays with each other,*
> *But once we did play with her brother.*

Eight-year-old Peter contributed this portrait of Eric:

> *He is the tallest in this school.*
> *He is not cruel.*
> *He has brown hair and brown eyes.*
> *He think he's wise.*
> *He lets you play with his football.*
> *That is all.*
> *(Who is he?)*

Eric blushed throughout the poem's delivery. The back-handed *He thinks he's wise* escaped his notice in the general gush of the tribute. I saw him at playtime give Peter a liquorice square as a token, we may take it, of royal favour.

Rhyme is obviously the first thing about poetry that catches the child's eye and ear. From there it is no small step to get him to beat out an organic rhythm or to select his words with real care. We do possess one home-made poem that shows some beginnings in this fastidious process; it was offered by eight-year-old, semi-literate Mavis. She asked me to write it down as she dictated it. It commemorates her sister's wedding which took place in the village. It goes:

> *Jill got married on Saturday*
> *And my father gave her away.*
> *Her dress was white and ever so nice*
> *But it was ever such a price.*
> *Mother cried and said to me,*
> *"Now Jill's gone the house will seem emp-ty."*

I suggested that an illustration of the wedding might also interest us; and this painting-and-poem of a homely event now has a place on the classroom wall. On reading the poem Mrs. Duckworth commented: "I'm glad to see somebody else cries at weddings besides me." There seem few events which do not bring in their wake a flood of foreboding to Mrs. Duckworth's soul; and weddings, more so even than funerals, do it in particular.

Though the writing of poetry, or the attempt to write it, can be a pleasurable and profitable activity its role in the task of awakening the young mind to "the ring of words" is a minor one. After all, there are children like Amy and Arthur who might sit stolidly in front of a blank sheet of paper and finish the afternoon by presenting one with nothing more fruitful than *The Birds and the flowers/Drink the showers* or something hardly less hackneyed. In such cases I would far sooner have them out before the class reading some poetry to me while livelier souls are writing it.

Equally repaying would it be to have them write down their thoughts in prose. A favourite poem of my children's is *Seumas Beg* by James Stephens, which Eric thought couldn't be a poem because of the ostensible absence of rhyme. I explained that the essential rhymes are there, but not apparent only because the poem reads more like what we think of as prose. Young children like their poetry not only to rhyme but to rhyme emphatically; and poems like *Seumas Beg* serve the salutary purpose of showing the older children who are ready for more varied adventures with words that the power and appeal in a poem may well lie elsewhere than in its rhyme.

It's here that stand-bys like Shakespeare and the Bible come into their own, so numerous are the passages in both that have not only beauty but the strength and simplicity to get across to children. A prayer much in use in my school are the lines of St. Paul to the Philippians:

Finally, Brethren,
whatsoever things are true,
whatsoever things are honest,
whatsoever things are just,

whatsoever things are pure,
whatsoever things are lovely,
whatsoever things are of good report;
if there be any virtue, and if there
be any praise, think on these things.

My fond hope is that long after my children have vanished
into the wide world, and perhaps forgotten much of what they
learned in school, they will sometimes recall the poems we read
together and will "think on these things".

MAKE-BELIEVE

BOVE all things, perhaps, the children in my school love to dress up. We own a large trunk filled to the brim with apparel of a bizarre kind: a top hat, paper hats from by-gone Christmas parties, curtains threaded with tape that transforms them into "cloaks", two pairs of beach pyjamas that have undeniably seen better days on the sands at somewhere like Rhyl, an embroidered waistcoat rescued from a jumble sale that Oscar Wilde might have coveted, three kimonos and innumerable other but less easily specified treasures.

When I first introduced these dressing-up clothes into school the children were so excited that they could think of no game to play with them, but instead donned them and strutted wildly about the hall, shouting to each other like "extras" trying to create "atmosphere" in an "historical" film.

Even the eldest, Eric and Amy, joined in: Eric in a top hat and beach pyjamas, Amy in a purple wrap and green veil over her dark head that gave her the appearance of some unwanted "remnant" in an Eastern slave market. Five-year-old Willie's fancy was a red corduroy dressing-gown in which he rolled convulsively about on the floor like a boxer who has been "fouled".

Once the first excitement was over and the notion of a trunk full of old clothes in school seemed perfectly natural, ideas for using them in a more purposeful way took root and began to flourish. These mostly centred about the Wendy House, which could be used as a palace or witch's cave according to what game was being played. At first a game would last an afternoon and a fresh one be devised next day, but we have now reached a routine where each child has its favourite clothes and, in most cases, its favourite "character"; and we play out regularly—in an unending sequence resembling the Gondal "sagas" invented by the young Brontë children—our own home-grown pageant.

Lethargic little Henry, for instance, is invariably what he calls "a magic man" in this game, six-and-a-half-year-old Edith tenaciously sticks to a long brown skirt that she seems to have adopted as though it were some kind of orphan, seven-and-a-half-year-old Beryl insists for some obscure reason that might (or even might not) fascinate a psychologist on squeezing herself into whatever game is played as a "bride", adorned for this touching role in a discarded piece of lace curtain originally owned by Mrs. Duckworth that she drapes round her shoulders. With her long, wistful face she looks less like a bride than some abandoned mother in a "heart-rending" Victorian melodrama whom you expect at any moment to stick her foot inside a pub door and sing "The Lips That Touch Liquor Shall Never Touch Mine"; but, happily, to her non-theatre-going classmates she looks what she says she is, so everyone is satisfied all round.

These games are entirely unsupervised or directed, so that there are occasions when the collective absorption is such that playtime has come and gone unheeded.

Snatches of dialogue reaching me at my desk carry strong hints of the variety of situations created:

Henry: I've killed you with a spell. You has to be dead.
Susan: No!
Six-and-a-half-year-old Edith: Yes, go on, you be dead and we'll bury you.

Seven-and-a-half-year-old Beryl: I'm the mother and I've just got married.
Five-year-old Colin: Can I be the father?
Beryl: All right, but you 'as to go to work while I gets the dinner ready.
Eight-year-old Mavis: You can't do that if you've just got married, silly! You 'as to go on your honeymoon. Now, go on, you go off on your honeymoon and I'll stay and look after the children.

Eric: Come on, you kids. I'm the teacher.
Arthur: When I knocks on the door you 'as to say, "Here's the doctor come to examine everybody."
Eric: They've got to sing hymns first.
Bystanders in chorus: "All things bright and beautiful . . ."
Eric: Henry, you has to pretend to come late for school.
Henry: No, I don't.
Eric: Yes, you has to. It's got to be like a real school!

The Wendy House and its appurtenances has given more enjoyment to the children than anything else. Even my few five-year-olds will participate with a concentration rarely granted any other activity. They mostly prefer to play together there while the older ones are occupied, and it is quite a sight to see them sitting round the little table, politely pouring out for each other water from the tiny teapot into the tiny cups, and serving each counterfeit cakes with a ceremonious solemnity that would not disgrace the proverbial vicar's tea-party.

Their world of make-believe is not limited to games in the Wendy House. They much enjoy, like all children, acting stories in collaboration. With so few of them there is, of course, scarcely anyone to spare for the role of audience on the occasions we do these collective and impromptu plays. I say "we" because I usually join them, regarding it as good practice for the teacher to participate in the children's dramatics; for in the Primary school, except on special occasions, producing can be done as the play goes along and it seems to create a far friendlier atmosphere when the teacher is one of a group of players than when she is merely watching operations from some vantage point.

Without denying that I am anything but what would be defined in the acting world as a "ham", I can nevertheless exhibit a far wider range of emotions than my children, and it does encourage them to be freer in gesture and speech when they see that *I* don't mind laughing or shouting in anger or gathering up my skirts and dancing a hornpipe (should the play unhappily call for it!).

Particularly tongue-tied and wooden are the Junior children when doing what they call "a proper play" (which is not the same thing as what the censor means by it!) that they feel demands decent speech and heavy characterisation. Not a single one of them has ever visited a theatre except for their annual pantomime, and their idea of an actor is the film hero in a Western who is tall in the saddle and quick on the draw or, in the case of the girls, the newest "blonde singing discovery".

I did not join in their drama with the intention of showing them what wonders could be achieved with, say, the part of Red Riding Hood; it all began with my slipping unobtrusively into minor parts as a stop-gap whenever there was a shortage of actors to go round. My first appearance on the boards was as one of the rats in *The Pied Piper of Hamelin*. From there I worked myself up to the role of the old witch in *Hansel and Gretel*, and I "arrived" on the day that Eric and I brought down the house as the two Ugly Sisters in *Cinderella*. From that day I have never, as they say in acting circles, "looked back".

Without my intending it I have become typed as a kind of female Boris Karloff, my closest rival in the field being Eric who greatly fancies himself as unrivalled in sadistic roles, like that of a wolf, giant or some other kind of evil genius, that so plentifully pepper children's stories.

Our drama takes place on the floor of the hall, the use of dressing-up clothes and props left entirely to the children's fancy. The little ones prefer, when possible, to play out their stories with the Juniors merely as an audience. Without such an occasional indulgence they would tend to be swamped by the more pronounced personalities of the older children; but they do, as well, like to participate in those stories that the whole school play together. The informality of the occasion is, of course, accentuated most helpfully by the small numbers engaged and is a good minor example of the contemporary drama-in-the-round.

Although the children are aware of little except the enjoyment they are deriving from the drama, it is obviously necessary that the teacher should be noting the progress, if any, they are making in it. Here is an important distinction between their own entirely free play and the enacting of stories already told them: for in the latter activity they are learning something about the use of language and gesture, about co-operation in the cause of a collective creation and learning too the discipline necessary for that creation.

Though it goes without saying that child drama should, like child art, be free, live and vigorous, it may not generally be understood that the growth of these qualities without the help of a teacher who incorporates them in her basic attitude is most unlikely. Nothing so helps this attitude, it's my experience, than the teacher's participation in the children's drama.

Five-year-old Willie, uncontrolled and regarded as a nuisance when he throws himself galvanically into whatever story is being played, is beside himself with joy when I take his hands and say: "Come on, Willie, you and I will be goblins together, shall we? Where shall we hide till the Princess comes?"

Ten-year-old, shy Amy flushes with pleasure when I put my arm round her shoulders and suggest: "I think we should do very well as the two farmers' wives. Let's go and find an apron each."

There are many such children who can never get all they might from a game of make-believe—through shyness or some other inhibition—who will profit from an adult's help in the way described; and the adult concerned will incidentally be helped towards a more sympathetic understanding of the particular handicaps of the child with whom she is sharing a role in the drama.

As well as the problem of getting the most out of enacting stories there are the stories themselves to consider. I never tell the children a story with the thought or object in my mind: "We shall be able to act this afterwards." Should they enjoy hearing the story and wish to work it out again through the medium of drama I am only too pleased; but the wish to do it must come from them.

Sometimes, instead of acting out the story in a conventional way, two or three children will prefer to dramatise it with the aid of puppets—to the delight of the rest who never tire of being an audience for our home-made puppet theatre.

Particularly successful results have been obtained with tales such as *The Cat and the Jar of Yellow Butter*, *The Golden Goose* and some of the Brer Rabbit stories. There are children who are never so happy and free with speech as when enunciating it through puppets and concealing their own shy identity.

As an aid to the awkwardness of speech and gesture of such children has been my introduction of them to miming. Their start in it was made with the story of *Jack and the Beanstalk*. The whole group of them took turns in playing each character in the story, and it was performed without music. They were encouraged particularly to try and get the "feel" of the angry giant, the saddened mother of Jack, the giant's timorous wife and daring young Jack himself.

I commended eight-year-old Mavis for a light-handed interpretation of Jack's character and her real-life imitation of his escape down the beanstalk, to which she rejoined: "You can think about what he's like better when you haven't got to say anything, can't you?"

After several try-outs the children were divided into groups: one to practise playing the giant, one to do Jack, and so on, and it was all mimed once again. Here the distinctions in size between the children contributed an unexpected novelty to the story. All the little children played Jack, the five biggest boys played the giant, and the girls divided up the women's parts among themselves.

An interesting result was that the Infants kept breaking into involuntary speech, showing perhaps that miming is not as suitable for them as for the older ones. They found it far more natural, when playing Jack, to say "Good-bye" to Mother before clambering up the beanstalk, and they preferred to ask the giant's wife, "Will you give me a drink of water?" to miming the request. So our miming, except when it is accompanied by music, has scraps of conversation thrown in for good measure.

Although I believe that child drama should be a spontaneous creation we do like to produce during the term one simple play to which parents can be invited. I think this is particularly necessary because my children lack the advantage of those in a large school who would be able to invite the class next door or the rest of the Infant or Junior school to witness a performance. This is one of the real advantages of a large school, and we try to compensate for it by having the parents present to supply the applause and appreciation. They will consist chiefly of mothers—for the performance is a matinée one!—and for it programmes are compiled and distributed, a back-cloth is painted to lend a spice of realism to our improvised stage and the dressing-up clothes are pressed and, if necessary, repaired by Juniors in the kitchen under the surveillance of Mrs. Duckworth.

She is astonished to see boys pressing and stitching clothes, and assures me that "it's more than they'd do for their mothers", but she charitably (if mystifyingly) puts it all down to "this modern education".

The advantage in such a small school as ours is that everyone can play in the performance. I recall a similar occasion in a large city school where there were fifty-two children in my class, and being advised by a colleague who was an "old hand" at this kind of thing to "always choose a play with a forest in it, and then anyone for whom a part can't be found can be a tree".

It is far pleasanter to dispense with "trees", as I am able to do here, for I have never been happy about children who play the part of a tree. I think they suspect that the play has no real need of them. When I mentioned this to the colleague who had advised the improvisation she replied: "You're too sensitive, my dear. As long as the Mums can see their little darlings on the stage, it's all that matters."

I think, however, I was right about this when I recall my own days as a schoolgirl. Those children who were not playing the part of a tree could always, up to the very eve of the performance, be brought to heel for misbehaviour by the teacher, by a reminder that there were only too many children in the class due to play the part of a tree who would be glad to change places with them if they didn't watch their step. . . .

An unfortunate attitude on the teacher's part: it tended implicitly to stress a distinction—so widely current in the professional theatre—between the "stars" and the rest. Very often, I recall, one's part in a play depended more on how one behaved in class than on the really relevant factors; so that "bad" boys were invariably demoted to being "trees" and were sometimes even displaced from that little theatrical niche on account of inability or disinclination to hold their "branches" still—giving one the impression of some juvenile version of Birnam Wood shuffling off to Dunsinane.

STORY TIME

SEVEN-YEAR-OLD Susan brings a paper-backed booklet to school.

"Would you read us this story, it's ever so good?" she says.

The product she put into my hand was of a very garish order. It illustrated the adventures of a certain "Loafie the Lion" who owed his survival among equally powerful beasts in the jungle to his shrewd expedient of arranging to be asleep whenever trouble was about.

The illustrations can be best described as being of a tenth-rate Disney variety; and Disney at his worst at that. The dialogue was largely a matter of Yahs, Yippees and Shurrups. I looked up from the book to Susan's eager face, and she repeated: "Will you read it to us?"

This type of request must, I am sure, confront all Primary teachers from time to time. How do you answer the child who makes it? Say right out: "This book is dreadful, fit only for lighting the fire?"

No, you can't say that. Nor can you obviously do the opposite: read the book to the class.

One usually falls back on some excuse like: "It's really too long for us to read in school," or "I don't think it's a very suitable book for me to read to the children, dear," or one simply wriggles out of it by the unanswerable edict: "We already have a story for this afternoon," and hopes devoutly that the request won't be made again next day.

I can't help asking myself at such times: Why do people publish these booklets? I am sure a good sale can be achieved with illustrations that are not crude and degrading. I have never in my life met a child who was bored with a story because it was written in good English.

It's true that from the sales point of view these booklets are inexpensive, in that they are produced on a strip-cartoon basis, but I am convinced that they do a great deal of harm, not because they are classifiable as "horror"—they certainly are not—but because they introduce and solidify standards of taste and behaviour that are appallingly low. Isn't it odd that in England the works of genius are often prosecuted in law for their imagined tendency to "deprave the young" while at the same time the products of unmistakably depraved minds are granted a free licence to be disseminated by the million? The worst of it all is that these products are almost always read chiefly by those children in drastic need of help in the raising of their standards.

It's no difficult matter to recognise books of this kind and to refrain from using them in school. They are notably what the late George Orwell meant by "bad" books. Not anything like so easy to detect are those for which he coined the ingenious label "good bad" books; these are books competently written but conspicuously without "guts". They are the type of book in which the author will never use the word "rabbit" where the word "bunny" is conveniently to hand; he is psychologically related to that school of newspaper writing to whom all children are "kiddies". Such books are pleasantly produced, pleasantly if unexcitingly illustrated, and of course popular.

As literature for children they are valueless, in the way that the tales in the "glossy" magazines are valueless as literature for their mothers. They are neither connected with what we would call "real life" nor with what we can concede is "real imaginative life"; they exploit the *naïveté* of children identically in the way the parent product exploits the *naïveté* of housewives.

Children are but too ready to "suspend disbelief" in the cause of pixies, gnomes or magic on account of their seeing the world we inhabit as a vast, mysterious place where anything (or anyone) can happen; but magic and magical beings should be related, according to their inherent principles, to real life, as they most certainly are in the old folk-tales where they so vividly and memorably represent the titanic forces of good and evil.

It is so easy to tell stories to children in which fairies and wood-land folk live in quaint little houses; any competent writer with no taste or conscience could do it, and many of course do (as their super-tax accounts with the Inland Revenue authorities could bear witness). Everything in these tales is utterly "cosy" and the children who listen to them chant "Ooh!" and "Ah!" as the words flow from the reader's lips in a treacly trickle; and a good time is had by all.

The fact is, these pathetic mites have been given no diet of good red meat but a soft, cloying pudding that vitiates the taste it satisfies. There is no point in denying that children love these stories as much as they would love any other kind, in the same way that they will eat an ounce of mouldy all-sorts with the same relish that they will consume chocolate liqueurs, but a child who is given nothing but mouldy all-sorts is often likely to grow into an adult whose taste in food, books, furniture, clothes and what-ever else bears the stamp of his early forms of nourishment. To give children "what they like" is to encourage the mentality of the pig-swill trough into which whatever is thrown is gobbled up with the same indiscriminate voracity.

Whether or no there is a place for this kind of reading in the home, there can surely be none for it in any unit genuinely concerned with education. Story time in school is one of the most precious of all periods in the curriculum. Teacher and children should be sitting quietly together, sharing a beautiful hour in the wonder of a story. Here is no learning-by-doing, no particular aspect of Free Activity. The children are simply coming into their birthright: a splendid tale well told.

I always try—as in the reading of poetry—not to superimpose my own personality on that of the author's. Good stories will very often contain words or phrases that puzzle the children, and I sometimes explain them beforehand or after the story is read; never do I stop to haggle over them in the middle of the telling. Think how easy it would be to ruin that enchanting opening of Beatrix Potter's tale about the Flopsy Bunnies by a halt in the reading to ask: "Who knows what *soporific* means?" and when (obviously) nobody does, to add: "Well, it means something that makes you sleepy."

This type of story-telling is likely to result in making the children sleepy, too. . . .

You can only befog children who, of course, have never heard of lettuce making one sleepy, and as an explanation is in any case made redundant by the author herself who uses the word in this self-explanatory context: "I have never felt sleepy after eating lettuces; but they certainly had a very soporific effect on the Flopsy Bunnies."

The description, of course, conforms to its own inner laws in that, I should guess, it is rooted in old country saws, and the most sceptical child will soon find himself quite ready to believe, while immersed in the story, that lettuce leaves would have the same effect on *him* lying on a dozy summer's afternoon on Mr. McGregor's rubbish heap.

So with the children sitting round me on their rush mats I

read to them the saga of the Flopsy Bunnies and show them the pictures—and trust the language to look after itself.

Reading stories to a group of children with a five-to-eleven age range may at first mention seem a form of mental acrobatics rather than a serious item in their education. This impression would be justified were the older children as "sophisticated" as are usually their urban counterparts; but Amy, Eric and Arthur are markedly naïve and untutored in comparison with city Juniors, and they find an unmixed appeal in listening to the very simple stories told to the Infants, even though they have their own choice in stories later in the afternoon when the Infants have gone home.

They don't have to come and listen to stories told specially to the Infants. There are, of course, on occasion stories chosen that do have a genuine all-age appeal. My choices differ greatly from one another; samples are *Catskin* by the Brothers Grimm, Edward Ardizzone's *Tim* stories, Elizabeth Clark's *Pussy, will you have a sausage?* or the Brer Rabbit tales, or some of those collected by Andrew Lang, or the lovely Pére Castor stories.

My children, with the possible exception of eight-year-old Peter, and Kate, are not "easy" readers (and not even Peter and Kate—who are—have anything like exhausted the supply of school books in stock), so that the more they listen to stories the better, I feel, it is for them.

The bookcase is of a type that holds two or three books on each of its ledges with the front cover of the book put to face the borrower. About twelve books can be held in the case in this way and I change them once a week. As most of them are books I have read to the children it is possible for even the youngest to take them out, pore over them and have a pretty successful try at retelling the stories in their own words.

I have sometimes overheard children like Edith and Susan telling these stories so fluently that I have suspected them—unfoundedly, I should add!—of reading straight out of the book.

As most of these books are expensive it is generally appreciated that special care must be taken in handling them, and the routine of washing one's hands before picking up a book has long been established without fuss. I think it far better to spend a little time on this business connected with the handling and reading of books than keeping them on a special inaccessible shelf labelled "Teacher's books".

Most of my children have never before in their lives held in their hands or scrutinised at their leisure attractively produced books. Added to the awesomeness of this privilege is an insight into the financial implications provided for them by the knowing Eric or Mavis telling them in reverently hushed tones: "That book costs fifteen shillings. It says so. Look!"

They can understand fifteen shillings spent on a mechanical toy or a cowboy suit—but on a book? Seven-and-a-half-year-old Bernard voices their astonishment in the terse understatement:

"Well, I'm blowed!"

There is an aspect of story-telling which, while without pretensions to being literature, does both delight them and make demands on their imagination.

This consists of the stories they and I invent about ourselves. Sometimes the story is a very short one, sometimes it stretches over three or four lessons as a kind of serial. A favourite one of this type which is added to in each retelling is the one about Eric and his aeroplane. Eric is (naturally!) the pilot. Arthur and Peter are the crew. Mavis is the air hostess. The rest of us are the passengers. The plot consists of the adventures we have travelling in the aeroplane.

We have crashed into the sea, Henry has only narrowly escaped being swallowed by a whale (due to Eric's breath-taking skill with a harpoon), we have flown to Africa to prove to Edith that bananas do just grow on trees; and while there a monkey crept into the aeroplane without our knowledge and disrupted the crew by throwing nuts at Peter.

It's I who usually begin the story and the children who add to it as the fancy takes them. I am not sure how it would all work out with a large class, but here it goes with an effortless swing. I often overhear the children retelling the story to one another afterwards in small groups, with themselves of course replacing the others in the chief parts. . . .

In the summer we cross into the fields opposite the playground for story time and there, among the Cotswold hills and isolated greystone farm-houses, the reading of a story in the still sunshine takes on, it has sometimes seemed to me, almost a mythological quality as though our little group was an arrangement of figures eternally captive in some framed landscape. When I read *The Wind in the Willows* beside a small stream up on the hills, a half-mile or so distant from school, my words dropped among them in a hush so electric that I don't think a single eyelid would have batted in surprise had Rattie and Mole actually appeared before us.

MUSIC AND MOVEMENT

F sixteen children in my school two have a piano at home and one an harmonium. One mother—Susan's—can play the piano. The harmonium is owned by five-year-old Doris's family, who are of a pietistic turn of mind and have hopes that Doris will learn to play the instrument in due course.

At present the children know no music other than what they have heard in school. This includes "tinkling" on the piano (for which eight-year-old Peter has a particular *penchant:* he has taught himself to play the tune *Jack and Jill*); learning time values with the aid of coloured charts and percussion instruments; and, in the case of the oldest Juniors, learning to play the simpler hymns on the recorder at Morning Assembly.

I am myself moderately musical. I can sing in tune, play un-complicated music on the piano, and what I know of recorder playing has been learned in co-operation with the children. I enjoy listening to music and what I lack in technical appreciation is atoned for to some extent, I like to hope, by my enthusiasm.

There is no gramophone in school, but there is a wireless set, and in a scrutiny of the *Radio Times* I often find first-class record-ings of music suitable for my children to listen to. As these recordings are not officially part of the "Schools Programme", and consequently irregular in their occurrence, we have, if we wish to listen to them, to drop whatever we are doing and gather round the wireless.

The little ones sometimes hear the music only as a background —when it is not suitable for them—to some quiet activity they may be pursuing. They have all in their time listened often to such pieces as Tchaikovsky's *Nutcracker Suite*, Elgar's *Nursery Suite*, Tchaikovsky's *Waltz* from *The Sleeping Princess* and Walton's *Façade*.

While this kind of thing is obviously of value—besides showing them that the wireless also provides music other than that pur-veyed by dance bands and variety—what I particularly like to provide is "live" music. Soloists prepared to cut into their precious time to visit an isolated village school do not grow on trees, but a determination to get hold of a performing artiste from time to time can do wonders. We have had a visit from a violinist, oboist and clarinettist.

With a small group like ours we were able to sit closely to these players and "share" their instruments in a way that would be unrealisable in a big school. The children, it was apparent, were itching to get their fingers on the instruments but, unhappily, their privileges stopped short of this.

Such visits are the high-spots in their musical education.

Singing presents special problems of its own in a group so small as ours. For example, both nine-year-old Arthur and seven-and-a-half-year-old Bernard have powerful voices that would shame a corncrake into silence, and there is simply no chance of their just being lost in the crowd. There they always are, croaking away, full of goodwill and bad notes. I used to wonder how aware of it other children were, when one afternoon Mavis turned to Bernard who stood beside her, giving his all, and said: "You don't arf shout and you hasn't got the tune right, either." Bernard raised the most astonished eyebrows I have ever seen. He could not have been more taken aback had he been accused of not breathing correctly. The way he sees it is: he's been singing all his life and nobody's complained before. Why should Mavis suddenly pick on him? It just shows you what girls are!

As I happen to know that controlled breathing and controlled singing are closely related, I have been able to help him and Arthur to become more "acceptable"—musically speaking—but with all I can do for them they are still a long way from the prospect of finding themselves invited to Glyndebourne.

I would never throw out the "droners" from communal singing simply because they spoil the tune for, given time, they do learn to modify their voices and to that extent improve their singing; very few children are ever found to be tone-deaf. Their only chance of improving their singing is, after all, in the opportunity to sing in the company of children who sing well.

I try also to have as much singing without a piano as with one. The piano, I sometimes think, can be more of a hindrance than a help with young children, and I never resort to it unless I am so familiar with a song that I can play it on the piano and look at the children at the same time.

When the weather permits we sing out of doors in the play-ground. Surely children are much closer to the spirit of Morning Assembly when they can sing a hymn like *Glad that I Live Am I* by Lizette Reece or Eleanor Farjeon's *Morning Has Broken* under a blue sky and in the midst of tall poplar trees. Our playground is small, but with an excellent surface and in a good position for both sun and view.

In such conditions—and there are more bright mornings even in our English climate than most people will concede—Arthur and Bernard are more easily forgiven for their voices. We get some odd visitors on these occasions in the small children who are nearly old enough to begin school and spend a lot of their time yearningly hanging about the gate. Among them are sometimes old men born and schooled in the village, who lean over the wall goggle-eyed at these modern goings-on. And if the postman arrives in the middle of it all he will hand me the post with a wink and a mock-wistful, "Wish I was still at school!" There is always an audience of some kind, even if it's only Mrs. Duckworth's cat squatting on the school wall and thinking her thoughts about all this.

During the Physical Education period that we have once a day there will be, weekly, our wireless "Music-and-Movement" programme, and one other period of music-and-movement that I take to the accompaniment of the piano and the percussion instruments. Although the age range is so wide the Physical Education periods work out quite well along "free" lines. While, for example, the younger ones are experimenting with balls and skipping ropes involved in the—for them—complex business of bouncing a ball and learning to skip, the older children will be absorbed in subtler forms of ball-and-rope play.

We use as much improvised apparatus as I can think of: jumping over obstacles of varying size, clambering over the Cotswold stone wall that hedges in the playground, swinging by the hands from the lintel of the door that in the bad old days was the place where we kept the "bucket", scrambling through an old clothes-horse held steady by two children.

In the field opposite the school are a couple of trees most appropriate for climbing which have low branches that offer safe support. A popular pastime this; even fragile little Lily and Doris work up a thrill in clutching the branches and swinging them-selves about on it, Tarzan fashion.

Perhaps I am less distantly removed from my ancient ancestors than I ought to be at this point in time, but I confess to quite an urge to try my luck at scaling the trees in company with the children. The thought of village opinion (and my silk stockings) is all that deters me from unrestrained participation, although there was an occasion when I got halfway up the "easiest" of the trees on the pretext of helping six-and-a-half-year-old Edith get down from it.

This urge to join in can be more conveniently exercised when we are indoors during our music-and-movement periods. These include free interpretation of music or rhythms and group dancing and miming. Sometimes I play the piano for the children as they dance and mime some story or activity: a circus, a walk in the jungle or—to come nearer home—a football match.

How vastly they enjoy interpreting the animals in the jungle to the music of Saint-Saëns! A dance of this kind lends itself to sequences of an endless variety, an example on one occasion being an imaginary fight between two lions played by Eric and Peter. In criticising them I said: "It's no use just fighting, you must try to let the music help your fight."

"But that means," protested Eric, "that we can't fight properly!"

"I don't want you to fight properly," I replied. "I want you only to look as though you are fighting properly. That's quite another thing!"

This didn't exactly please Eric who saw himself in the role of a lion rampant, but when he did try to work out this calculated and directed kind of battle with the help of the music he found it less of a "sell" than he'd imagined. His and Peter's gestures were stiff and awkward at the beginning, but practice soon brought quite creditable results.

As well as dance-and-mime to set pieces of music I try to encourage the children to move to music of their own making. This might often involve nothing more startling than rhythmic patterns and tone, but it is sufficient to provoke interesting results.

They may, for instance, be given a tambourine and off they go beating it and moving quite freely about the room in response to their accompaniment. If there are not enough tambourines to go round those without them will find clapping the hands a very good rhythmic basis for this type of free movement.

Mavis, in many ways a slow, heavy girl, responded to the invitation with surprising agility and inventiveness. She said: "I've seen a girl dancing with a tambourine on the pictures," and in imitation she bent and swayed her body in the way she had seen the trained dancer do it—at the same time banging the tambourine on her elbows and knees as well as with her hand. The other children watched her, caught up—as children invariably are by someone else's enthusiasm.

Mavis stopped half-way through the dance and said: "You really wants bells on your ankles."

"Yes, why not?" I said, and with the aid of string we tied a pair of Indian handbells to her ankles, which delighted her and her audience as she went off twisting and twirling to the sound of bells and the hammering of the tambourine.

It is a pity that our schoolroom floor isn't smooth enough for the children to dance barefoot on it, and they have to wear plimsolls, but in the warm weather we are able to use a near-by field for barefoot dancing. I had never taught children under such conditions before, and it makes the best hall seem a poor makeshift in comparison. Limitless sky and fresh air have a releasing effect on us all, the very youngest children being no exception; in the open air they dance with an energy and abandon that I, at least, have never succeeded in exacting from them indoors.

They will not only be barefoot for this occasion but very scantily clad in general. It is an experience as new for them as it is for me. They take surroundings such as these for granted, as city children take narrow streets and smoking chimneys, but apart from traditional activities like helping the farmer at hay-making or scaling a tree for birds' eggs, their intimacy with the country in which they live is, I have found, very limited.

There may have been a time when children here were brought up to dance round the maypole and to be able to sing what we would regard as an enviable number of folk-songs, but if this was so the march of civilisation has certainly put a stop to it. The only dancing they do now is a kind of jig to the accompaniment of a dance band on the wireless and their singing is restricted to what are called, I believe, "hot numbers".

Perhaps this section could be suitably closed with a note on the type of song I choose for my children. For the younger ones there are, of course, the nursery and simple folk-songs. If, by way of variety, I have selected songs that are words set to the music of folk-songs of other lands I try to be careful to pick only worthy translations of them. Far better let the children enjoy hearing and perhaps learning to sing a song like *Au Clair de la Lune* in its original than—because it is an attractive tune—fit it to English words that are no more inspiring than:

> *The bright moon is shining,*
> *Peter, my dear friend.*
> *For your pen I'm pining,*
> *Say that it you'll lend,* etc.

The above may be one of the very worst of English versions, but I have met a disconcertingly large number of foreign folk tunes set to insipid English words.

The Juniors have singing lessons late on one or two afternoons after the Infants have left school, and on these occasions they sing songs and do work on the theory of music in a fashion not suitable for the younger ones.

Both Juniors and Infants sing together, too; songs like *What shall we do with a Drunken Sailor? The Drummer and the Cook, Billy Boy,* to mention only a few songs with choruses. The Juniors sing the verses and the younger ones join the chorus; which works out in the Juniors not singing songs too young for them but which nevertheless contain variety enough to justifiably include the Infants. Percussion instruments and recorders are used on these occasions, when they give additional pleasure.

Yes, pleasure. It is, I suppose, the key-word to all music-and-movement in the Primary school. The more that children delight in the varied aspects of this subject the more they will put into it, and that means the more they will get out of it.

Here as in no other subject is the teacher combating a positive opposition, for in the homes of many Primary children cheap canned music and singing are the accepted background to family life.

I don't after all my efforts expect Eric to go home and tell his parents: "Aw, turn that rubbish off—let's hear some Bartok!" What *is* possible, perhaps only barely possible, is that a seed has been planted and that when a listener on, say, Family Favourites puts in a request for the Polovtsian Dances from *Prince Igor*, Eric may announce to an unheeding family: "Shut up, everybody, I wants to listen to this. We heard it in school."

THE SOCIAL GROUP

HAVE had the experience in my day of supervising a hundred children eating school dinners in a disused chapel. It was not a pleasant duty. I don't imagine the children found it any pleasanter than I did. There were present none of the "refinements" we associate with the consumption of food in civilised surroundings: table-cloths, pots of flowers, conversation with one's neighbour.

The atmosphere could be almost chemically diagnosed as comprising fifty per cent yelling, fifty per cent mechanical clatter. It reminded me of Hollywood films I have seen of the inside of Sing Sing with the convicts being depicted in an ugly mood.

Amidst it all could be heard the occasional despairing wail of a teacher, like that of someone lost inside a tomb appealing for help: "Do please try to make less noise, children!"

It may have been a useful exercise for the teacher's lungs, but it was not an effective method of bringing to naught the consequences of a hundred knives and forks being thrust into action, and a hundred pairs of feet pattering across the floor. The notion behind this monster meal service of it becoming the basis of "social training" never escaped from merely being an idealist's day-dream.

Yet under fair conditions dinner at school can justify itself as a basis for social training and be a pleasant part of the school day into the bargain. In my school dinner-time is precisely an enjoyable break between two periods of school work.

I shall not pretend it's a financial success as well! Heavy subsidies, we all know, keep this scheme solvent, but in the case of my school we do at least get a return for the money.

The dinners are cooked in a small kitchen leading off from the school Hall by Mrs. Duckworth who is busy in there from nine-thirty onwards every day. The number of children for whom she cooks varies from between nine and twelve, and there are, of course, both Mrs. Duckworth and myself to be included in the day's catering.

Mrs. Duckworth's own description of herself is that of a "good, plain cook", a claim that opens up avenues of fascinating speculation, but I myself would place the emphasis on the "plain". Conscientiousness, for what it's worth, is Mrs. Duckworth's abiding virtue in the kitchen. She would never skimp or cut down on her cooking time to gain private leisure; yet oddly her cooking would be all the better for it if she did.

At present she rolls up her sleeves at nine-thirty and seems to feel that she is really earning her money the sooner she can fill her little kitchen with the merry sound of bubbling water and the homely aroma of boiling cabbage. She believes in cooking food until there is not an ounce of "fight" left in it, and has no sympathy with all this new-fangled stuff about vitamins and raw food which she suspects is a theory concocted by people who can't or won't cook properly. She is too tactful to as good as tell one so to one's face, but it's evident that where cookery is concerned her motto is: by their deeds shall ye know them.

The children eat Mrs. Duckworth's food, all except her rice pudding. She has at last given up making it. There was nothing actually wrong with it apart from its being hard (if you can call that "nothing"). Once when I politely refused it she commented: "Mrs. Whittle, the last headmistress, never cared for rice pudding, either." Mrs. Duckworth believes that she has given up making rice pudding because no one likes rice pudding; I'm content to leave it at that.

For the rest her meals are quite popular, and if I personally don't eat all that she puts before me it's accounted for by my dainty appetite: a legend that I allow to persist as long as it makes everybody happy.

Like all the cooks I have known Mrs. Duckworth has her favourite food. In her case it is beetroot. She has the same relationship with beetroot that the Restoration fop had with snuff: she always has some about with her. As a result the rest of us can't get away from it, either. We find it on the dinner-table as punctiliously as we find the condiments there. It is served with stew, with shepherd's pie, with roast beef, and it's particularly plentiful when salad is on the menu; and whatever else has been eaten there is always a heaped-up plate of it on the kitchen table for anyone who wants to help himself when dinner is over. You might conclude that Mrs. Duckworth earns a commission on each slice of beetroot consumed from some wholesale beetroot purveyor, but you would be wrong. She actually likes beetroot. It may not be a thing we care to believe about a fellow citizen, but these frightening truths have to be faced.

I get some on my own plate on most days, in spite of the fact that I nearly always leave it. One day it wasn't served and I thought with humble gratitude: "Ah, she realises at last that I don't care for it." Not on your life. Mrs. Duckworth appeared soon and announced with a face grave with tidings of sorrow:

"Beetroot's off this week. None to be had anywhere."

I did my best to look crestfallen.

The reasons I don't personally criticise Mrs. Duckworth about these things is firstly because it's a small price to pay for peace and harmony, and secondly because she is so humble and obliging a person, basically. She is still able to laugh over an incident that happened on the first day I took up my duties in school. She had brought me a mid-morning cup of cocoa that I found salty but nevertheless drank without a murmur of protest. . . .

Some two seconds later Mrs. Duckworth thrust a red, embarrassed face round the kitchen door and said: "I'm sorry, I made cocoa with the water I put ready for the vegetables and it had salt in it!"

I simply handed her back the cup without flinching.

"Fancy your not saying anything!" she said.

I smiled and replied: "I took it to be an old Cotswold custom to make cocoa with salt instead of sugar, and I like to keep up with the times."

Cooking conditions apart Mrs. Duckworth is a great help to have about the school. She is also admirable in restraining herself from gossip with me—unless I initiate it—when I am trapped in the classroom with her on a rainy playtime; although an exception, a perfectly excusable one, may be made of Monday mornings for the following reason:

Mrs. Duckworth is addicted (it's the only word) to the kind of newspaper whose headlines can be read quite clearly by a short-sighted person from a distance of a hundred yards and are usually a variation of some screaming injunction or slogan like: "IS THIS MAN FIT TO LIVE?" or "WOULD YOU LIKE THIS TO HAPPEN TO *YOUR* DAUGHTER?" On Sundays in particular Mrs. Duckworth makes a real feast of these choice items, and she turns up on Monday morning chockful of civic virtue, hardly able to wait till playtime to get some of it off her chest.

She likes to begin her story in the middle, like this:

"I see they've caught that man!"

Cautiously, I inquire: "What man?"

"Don't you read the papers?"

"No."

It's an odd thing but I've told Mrs. Duckworth on many a similar occasion, in as inoffensive a way as I can, that I don't read "those" newspapers, but there is evidently something about this information that doesn't get through to her. Or perhaps she thinks it's a joke. So on she goes:

"Well, I'm glad they got him!"

Since the conversation is destined, whatever my wishes, to run its course I do my best to contribute to it helpfully, as follows:

"What did he do?"

Here I have touched off—to revert to political jargon—"dynamite": for Mrs. Duckworth, unknowing to herself, is less concerned with what he "did" than with enjoying an indignation consequent upon the act. She says, heatedly:

"It just isn't right! I mean to say, a girl that age——" Indignation robs her of her breath.

I repeat: "A girl?"

"Only sixteen an' all——"

"But surely——"

"The dirty beast!"

"But——"

"You see, you can't even take a walk in the woods these days!"

"But——"

"You're just not safe *anywhere*. . . ."

So it continues until the children are brought in from the playground and Mrs. Duckworth's seethings are transferred to the kitchen and lost in the steam of boiling cabbage.

When I am unavoidably busy the children can always take their troubles with confidence to Mrs. Duckworth.

I try to encourage them to be self-reliant and not spend their playtime running in to me on the mildest pretext. Mostly I am in the playground with them, but there are times when I cannot be. They should then be able to take care of themselves, and mostly can, particularly as they get a lot of sympathy and help

from "motherly" types like Amy and Mavis who are concerned
to see that I am not disturbed by over-fussy children when I am
busy indoors with a visitor.

Once when I appeared from the classroom to say good-bye to a
visiting music inspector I overheard Mavis telling near-spastic
Willie: "I've told you she's got a lady with her and you can't go
in!" Willie repudiated this loudly and Mavis, mustering all the
firmness in her, told him: "You has to do what the teacher says.
That's what the teachers are for—to learn you what to do." This
for some reason struck Willie dumb. Or perhaps it merely
baffled him. He gave no more trouble, anyway.

We have two playgrounds, separated by a brick wall and an
opening in which a gate had once functioned. There has been
talk of pulling down the partitioning wall to make one large
playground, but so far no move has been made to implement the
suggestion. I find the wall an advantage from the children's point
of view. The Juniors especially like to feel they have some
privacy as a group and *I* find it convenient to be able to tell someone on occasion: "If there is any more squabbling you will be
put in separate playgrounds until your tempers improve!"

As both playgrounds are more than adequate in size for the
number of children using them, there is no pressing need—if need
at all—to have them combined into one large playground.

The children in them are supervised there by Mrs. Duckworth
during their play period after dinner so that I can get a rest. When
it rains or is severely cold they are brought into school and encouraged to busy themselves with any activity they choose. This
may vary from persuading Mrs. Duckworth to read to them to
collectively making a "ship"—as they did during one bad period
last winter. For it they used one or two old chairs with a back
or a leg missing, several planks of wood left behind by obliging
contractors, and a large quantity of nails and newspapers. For
Mrs. Duckworth, an intrigued and startled onlooker, it was an
insight for the first time into why the school so often resembles a
large workshop rather than the usual conventional school.

Fortunately the hall is spacious enough to house these projects in various corners when the school needs to be neatly arranged: as, for example, when dinner is to be eaten.

For much of the school work the children's tables are put out in pairs so as to form a large square around which four children can sit. It's a useful pattern for dinner, too, and we stick to it. The tables are laid with flowered American oil-cloth and whenever possible a small pot of flowers, leaves or berries in the centre.

The Junior dinner-children take it in turns to lay the tables, and for some of them it is still a feat of a kind trying to remember where to place such pieces of cutlery as the pudding spoon and fork. You might encounter seven-and-a-half-year-old Bernard experimenting with various arrangements while at the same time attempting to evade the critical attention of Mavis who knows where everything ought to go and enjoys being scornful of those who don't.

In each child's place there is a blue plastic beaker for him to fill with water from a large jug on the table, and the Juniors have made for each one of them a simple table napkin and a papier mâché napkin ring. Each napkin has been embroidered with the user's initials or, in the cases where ability did not extend this far, with a few coloured stitches that would identify the napkin for the user. None of them has ever used a table napkin before, and I'm sure that no hardened diner at the Ritz feels more "exclusive" than they do as they swish out the napkin from the ring with a flourish and spread it across their knees.

It's a pity they can't be persuaded to use the napkin for catching errant crumbs. Their one aim seems to be to keep it unsoiled. They tend to wipe mouths with a handkerchief, fingers or sleeve rather than sully the napkin. They will, however, take the napkin for granted some day and make more use of it.

Individual possessions of this kind are an incentive to personal pride and so to good manners. We are also fortunate in having an individual hand-towel for each child. These hang on pegs in the cloakroom. Above each peg is the user's name and, for the younger ones, a picture symbol to aid recognition. Here the children wash their hands before sitting down to dinner.

Two Juniors do dinner-duty on a rota. Mavis, who is a "regular" for dinner, particularly likes serving it to others. It may be connected with her having a sister who is a waitress in a tea-shop in a near-by town. Mavis brought one of her sister's discarded aprons to school one day, and ever since has been doing dinner-duty in style, augmenting the apron with a pretty white cap that she herself made in the needlework period.

There are the inevitable food faddists—here as elsewhere. Peter doesn't like custard, Arthur doesn't like cabbage, Willie doesn't like gravy. Sometimes children are difficult about food on account of being allowed to be so at home, like five-year-old Colin who, like his parents, will drink nothing but mineral water! Sometimes a child genuinely does not like a certain food. Our rule is that you must have a little of everything, which works out in a child having perhaps only a teaspoonful of a food he doesn't like. This is generally accepted by the children as a fair enough arrangement, though in practice there will sometimes be an attempt to get round it.

In such strategems Mrs. Duckworth's motherly instincts often lead her into complicity; but not so in the case of the dinner-servers! "Head Boy" Eric keeps a particularly eagle eye open for potential defaulters, and when he is on dinner-duty you can hear him swooping down heavily on them: "She" (*she* again!) "says you has to have a bit of everything and you has to eat it up. You won't have no pudding till you do."

I don't mind any of this too much till the occasion when I myself am a defaulter! I feel rather like a chief constable who has been caught pilfering. I'm a bad example . . . and Eric is accordingly harsher in his strictures.

Mavis, however, who serves me when she is on dinner-duty, is a devout believer in one law for Jack and another for his master. She whispers to me on certain occasions: "Shall I get your dinner without onions?" Stoically—though a bitter enemy of onions—I shake my head; but Mavis, who must have closely studied the career of the Serpent in the Garden of Eden, and enjoys it more if there is some initial resistance on my part, goes off to bring back a dinner *sans* onions. She puts it down stealthily before me, and stares brazenly round at everyone else as though daring them to protest.

I feel I ought to say: "I think I really must have just a little bit of onion, Mavis," but I haven't the heart to dampen her sense of an intrigue triumphantly concluded.

I catch a hint of what it must feel like to have what the politicians call Real Power. No wonder it is said to corrupt!

THIS AND THAT

ALL the children have contributed to the compilation of a book called "People We Know". In it each of them writes whatever he wishes to about any person in the village. In the case of the younger children spelling and punctuation are not emphasised. The aim, in fact, has been to obtain a free expression of their ideas and feelings.

When completed the book was illustrated and bound and put on view for whoever in the village cared to come and read it.

Here are extracts:

Seven-and-a-half-year-old Bernard on the subject of Mrs. Duckworth:

One day I saw Mrs. Duckworth cook the food for the school dinners and she cooks the potatoes and cabbage and meat and beetroot and for the second helping she cooks jam pudding and banana and custard. She lives with her father (*Bernard's title for Mrs. D.'s husband!*) up in the village and his name is Mr. Duckworth. When the plates are dirty he washes up. Then he puts them on the shelf and they stay there till next day.

Henry, seven:
Mrs. Duckworth makes good dinners for the school and she makes good puddings as well. She sometimes have a broom to sweep the playground. When the Teacher is over at home having a rest Mrs. Duckworth does look after us.

Mavis, eight, on the subject of the Rector:
The parson has two dogs. He has a chestnut one and a black and white one. Every Sunday he goes to preach in the Church. Then he comes home and goes to two more Churches. He is fat and wears a black suit and a white collar. He wears black shoes. He lives in a house by himself with two dogs. He is going to take us to the pantomime on Saturday. He has ordered a bus and now he is going to try and get the seats filled. You have to go to the Church if you wants to go to the pantomime for nothing.

Elizabeth, six, writes about the Rector:
The Rector has a car and it is yellow and black. He has 2 dogs. They live in his house. He has a pair of striped trousers and a top hat. He has a Church. I go to Church.

Edith, six and a half, writes about newly arrived twins:
When Mummy washed the twins they started crying and then Mummy sat them in the bowl to stop them and they did not cry any more. She put their nighties on and the littlest has the bottle first. I wish I was a baby so I could have a bottle of milk. (*This last sentence has some interest in that it states a problem: since the twins' arrival Edith has been behaving in a babyish fashion both in school and at home where she has developed a habit of sucking two fingers, forming a lisp and yelling for anything she wants. What is unusual about this desire on her part to be a baby again and so win back her favoured position with Mother is that, unabashedly, she has written it all down.*)

Here is her brother, Bernard, on the twins:
My twins are named Clifford and Andrew. Sometimes I feed them in the afternoon while Mummy puts them in the pram to go to sleep.

When Clifford woke he began to cry so I put the wireless on and then you couldn't hear him so he stopped crying. When Andrew woke he had his bottle. They look very tiny and they haven't got much hair and you has to be careful not to drop them.

Here are some other family portraits:

Henry, seven, on his grandmother:
She comes down and helps our Mum wash the clothes and the tea-cups from the caff. We live in the caff. Granny has a little house and she lives with her husband. I go to her house and she gives me sweets and things.

Elizabeth, six, writes about her sister, Lily (five):
My sister has got a red cardigan. She has a grey skirt. She is 5. She is a good girl and plays with me. She has 2 dolls. She won't eat honey. Nor me. She likes to eat cake. Mummy does not let her eat a lot of cake.

Peter, eight, writes about his two sisters (above):
Elizabeth is six and Lily is five. They sleep together. Lily takes her teddy bear to bed. They have races at putting their clothes on and Elizabeth wins. After school they play with their pram. Every Sunday they go to Church. They hide behind the door when I come home and throws a ball at me. I ducked and the ball never hit me.

Here in reticent contrast is Colin, five, writing about his three-year-old sister:
Our little girl does not know any games. She only plays with me.

Here are two entries again by Elizabeth and her brother Peter on the same subject.

Elizabeth, six, on "Our Birds":
Daddy has got 7 birds and they are budgies. He has got a white owl. It lives in a cage. It eats meat. One of the budgies talks and says Pretty Joey. The other birds can't talk.

Brother Peter, eight:
My father has seven birds. Two of them are mine. I help him to clean the birds out and I get their water for them. Last year we went

up to feed the birds and I saw a bullfinch. We had a cock and a hen bullfinch. The cock died. So we put the hen in a trap cage and we caught a cock bullfinch and put it in with the hen. They made a nest and laid some eggs and they had four babies. The nest fell down and the babies got killed. They laid some more but the eggs were no good so Daddy broke them all. We kept the bullfinches. Then we sold them to Mr. Haynes. He gave us the budgerigars and we have got one that talks. He says "Pretty Joey".

Finally, nine-year-old Eric on the Rector:

The Rector is a kind man. He lets the boys go to his house for a club. He plays cards with them and sometimes the Rector wins. He has a picture in his hall and it is painted by an artist and it is about the Churchyard. It was painted a long time ago. I know because in the picture there is a big tree and there is not one in the Churchyard now. The Rector has a Morris car and he take the boys for rides in it. He lets the boys wash his car when it is dirty and once he took me in his car to the shop to get some wellingtons.

One day seven-and-a-half-year-old Beryl came to me and said: "I went to a wedding at the week-end. Do you want to hear about it?"

"Yes, love to," I said, "but let's pretend I am a long way away and you have to write me a letter telling me all about it."

Here is the "letter":

On Saturday morning we went up to Reding for a wedding. First of all we had our dinner and then we went up to Church and when we came out of Church we all threw confetty over the bride and then they had their photographs taken and then we all went to the wedding recepshun and it was in a hall by the church and we played Passing the Parsal and we had balloons. There was two men in the band and one lady in the band and there was dansing as well and then we all went home in the car. At the wedding I drunk 3 glasses of lemonade. We all stopped at Reding for the night and came home on Sunday night at 6 o'clock and then we went up to my Aunties. I played with my cousin's Meccano set. Then we went home. I went to bed and this morning I got up and came to school and I am here in the school now.

Another means of self-expression in school derives from those periods spent by the children and me in conversation.

We were listening to a story about Christmas on the school wireless, and when the story was over seven-and-a-half-year-old Bernard asked me: "Do reindeers fly, Miss?"

I don't like this kind of question. With so many other adults I am in the invidious position of never having come to a decision about what I shall tell children about Father Christmas.

While I was thinking of a suitable answer Eric cut in:

"Of course they don't!"

"Then how does Father Christmas get on the roof?" Bernard retorted.

With an impatient sigh Eric said: "There *isn't* a Father Christmas. It's just your Dad."

Bernard then appealed to my judgment. Eric awaited it with a glint in his eye that seemed to say, "We've got you now!"

Ten-year-old Amy also watched me closely—but, I felt, with sympathy for my predicament. . . .

I said at last: "Well, if you want there to be a Father Christmas, then, of course, there is one."

"See!" Bernard told Eric.

Eric looked at me with undisguised suspicion. I hastened to clear myself.

"When you grow too old to want to believe in Father Christmas," I said, "like Eric and me . . . well, then, he doesn't exist any more."

Amy smiled with relief at my narrow escape—or perhaps at my cunning? The others looked grim. An uncompromising Yes or No was wanted from me.

When I refused to be drawn further the argument was taken up among themselves. I sat back—so did Amy!—to listen.

Mavis threw down the gauntlet at Eric.

"If it's just your Dad, how does he have time to get to everybody's house?"

Contemptuously, Eric said: "It's not *my* Dad, it's everybody's Dad."

Five-year-old Willie could stand being silent no longer:

"My Dad isn't Farver Christmas. I saw Farver Christmas in a shop."

"So did I," said Bernard, shamefacedly accepting support from this inferior quarter.

Nine-year-old Arthur, preferring to come down on the side of the mighty, called out: "That's only a man dressed up!"

Willie retorted: "He gave me a dip. A little aeroplane, but I broke it."

Mavis told him: "Your Mum 'ad to pay for it. There's tickets for two-and-six, 'cause I had one."

Willie had already lost interest. All he knew was that he did actually see Father Christmas in a shop and seeing is believing.

Said Bernard: "I know *that* was only a man. But there is a real Father Christmas who comes down the chimney. Our Mum says there is."

Eric, ruthlessly: "It doesn't matter what your Mum says. There isn't a Father Christmas. Your Dad puts the presents in your sock while you're asleep."

Feeling this to be a little rough on Bernard I said to Eric: "If you don't believe in Father Christmas it doesn't mean you have to try and persuade everyone else not to. Bernard likes to believe in Father Christmas."

"Kids' stuff!" said Eric: his last word on the subject.

The real last word came, however, from seven-year-old Susan:

"Well, there *is* a Father Christmas, see! He keeps his clothes in our airing cupboard. I've seen 'em!"

FRIENDS OF THE SCHOOL

CONTEMPORARY methods of education are often sadly bewildering to parents. It seems to them that children don't strive anything like so hard as they themselves did at school, too great an emphasis seems to be laid on play and some ambiguous activities called "Free Expression", and yet in the midst of all this today's world, as we know, needs all and more than it can get from its citizens in the way of knowledge and specialised abilities.

Parents may then be forgiven for thinking: "It's all very well to enjoy school and have fun there, but are they really learning anything?"

If questions like this go unanswered—and let's admit that they mostly do—sooner or later what started out as a question changes by imperceptible but aggravating stages into an opinion. What began by being tentative ends up by being assertive. "Are they learning?" finishes up as: "There's too much play in school and not enough work!"

We know what happens to an opinion strongly held: the urge to communicate it becomes too powerful to withhold, and in the case of the opinion at issue here it eventually reaches the child who becomes aware that his teachers and parents do not see eye to eye over this business of his education.

Never was it less necessary for such a situation to exist than today when there is so much that co-operative parents can do towards enlarging and extending the scope of education—although the onus of unleashing this creative spirit rests on the teacher.

There are, of course, parents who will remain uninterested in the education of their children in the face of the most insistent cajolery that any teacher can muster, but I think the majority today are more than anxious to do their share if somebody would only show them how.

The most satisfactory way so far devised to show them how, is through the medium of the Parent/Teacher Association. If as a teacher all you do in the way of recruiting parents' interest in your school is invite them to an Open Day they will remain—however pleasantly the atmosphere strikes them—spectators and not participants.

I have taught in city schools where it was so difficult to make personal contact with parents that no matter how many written appeals and invitations were sent out to them to join the Parent/Teacher Association, the tiniest proportion of mothers and the complete absence of fathers were inevitably the net result.

In a village like mine where all such invitations are made personally by the teacher it is impossible for the parents to remain unresponsive. Our PTA therefore consists of all the mothers and a goodly half of the fathers. We meet once every two months for a couple of hours in the evening, and join in a discussion led by a visiting speaker officially connected with education or the care of children, and we end with tea and biscuits served by Mrs. Duckworth, the cleaner.

I am the secretary, the treasurer is the chairman of the managers (the Rector), seven-and-a-half-year-old Beryl's mother is president, and another mother and two fathers make up the rest of the committee.

All the school managers, even those without children at school, are members of the PTA. One of them, a farmer, said at the first meeting: "I've been a school manager for twenty years, but I've never till now had much of an idea of what goes on inside school."

The first duty of a Parent/Teacher Association is, as its name indicates, to link parents and teachers in the common cause of the children's welfare. A successful union of this kind is an excellent thing in a city school, but in a village school it can be the very life-blood of the place.

In my school it has meant for a start a source of funds other than what the Education Committee is permitted to supply; this in turn has meant the purchase of up-to-date apparatus, like a jungle gym, which the annual Capitation Allowance could never go to, and this in its turn has meant an ever closer partnership between school and parents in pursuit of these ends.

Village folk are, I believe, notoriously great fund-raisers when the inclination takes them. Whist drives, beetle drives, old-tyme dancing, jumble sales: these are the very stuff of village life. How pleasant when there can be a sequel to them in the form of new amenities for the children in school from profits made by the parents!

While it is tempting—or should one say irresistible?—to use the PTA as a fund-raising concern, it is, from some points of view, even more useful as a beneficent source of make-do-and-mend voluntary labour! It was on one such evening that Beryl's father designed and painted a doll's dresser for the Wendy House, someone else repaired the wheels of the Infants' trucks, another touched up the dressing-up clothes, and several other parents attended to broken hinges on cupboard doors and similar needs that would otherwise have gone unheeded.

On being given two looms by the Education Committee for the Juniors to experiment in weaving I suggested to the girls— who were specially taken with them—that their fathers might be interested in making a loom for them to use at home. The sequel was the appearance of three fathers at my door the next evening to ask if they could be allowed to go into school and see what it was I had "said they'd got to make. . . ."

I have found that children have a genius—if that's the word!— for turning the mildest of suggestions into an order. I try when possible to write out a message I want delivered to a parent, for otherwise parents tend to accept a verbal message from me coming through a child precisely in the sense it is handed to them! I mention this because it is as well to face the fact that between even the ideal teacher and the ideal parent there is bound to exist some slight but definite tension. Each represents authority in the child's life and each understandably thinks he knows what's best for it.

I try to be as sceptical about a verbal message sent me through a child by a parent as I hope the parent is at the mutilated versions of my own messages that get through to her. When Bernard comes to school with the greeting: "Our Mum says I got to stay in playtime 'cause I've got a cold," or Doris turns up with: "Mummy says I mustn't use clay any more, it's too dirty," or Mavis tells me: "Mother says I'm not to do Physical Education because I've cut my foot"—I try to remember that it is unlikely— nay, impossible!—that the perfectly natural requests of the mothers mentioned were initially worded in the form of the uncouth ultimatums in which they have finally reached me. It's the gist of the request that matters to the child—though I'm not sure that some don't enjoy giving what they hope is "an order" to the teacher for a change.

Of course it also works the other way round: they like seeing their parents "told where they get off" from me. I have had mothers visiting me at school, asking hurtfully: "What's all this about our Johnny saying that he's got to bring a shilling to school for a flag day?" or: "Our Betty says you told her she can't sit in school with her blazer on even if she's got a cold!" .

I'm sure that parents must often get from children the most gruesome reports about school, as so often the teacher gets from them equally gruesome reports about home. A close and creative relationship between school and home can, if it does nothing else, whittle down these alarming and harmful legends. Disappearing —if not yet without trace—are, I hope, the memories of those days when Mother strode into Tommy's classroom, with arms akimbo and sleeves rolled up, to set about Teacher; and disappearing with them, too, the necessity for Teacher to turn up in Court to justify her behaviour in class before the law. It is preposterous, when it isn't tragic, that these should be the outcome of activities aimed at producing what Francis Bacon termed "the full man".

It has been my experience that no school is as well run as it might be without the goodwill and help of its pupils' parents. It's a pity that many parents who would be ready to help have a deep-rooted conviction that school is school and home is home and never the twain shall meet. The reason it's a pity is that the school day is all too short and the classroom all too full (usually) for teachers to achieve single-handed all that the child deserves from them.

One of our most interesting PTA meetings was given over to a discussion of the ways in which home life could strengthen and consolidate schooling. It was soon evident in our school work how profitable had been the discussion, and that as a result of it many of the children had since been allowed to weigh and measure ingredients for Mother's cooking, had helped Father measure his plots in the garden, and contributed their meed to calculating the cost of seeds and plants.

Yes, there is a lot they can do that will both strengthen and advance their schooling, and bring their parents profit and themselves pleasure at the same time.

Older children can shop, make out bills and handle change; younger ones will be delighted to be set the task (though for ourselves we should think it insane!) of counting the stairs, window panes or rooms of the house.

Measuring material for curtains or clothes and calculating the cost may be a headache for us, but for them it's first-class practical arithmetic (of the sort they can never do enough of in school) and an exciting game at the same time.

Letter-writing to relations who live too far away to make frequent visits can be not only a useful and enjoyable activity for the child but a great kindness to its elderly relations. I would stress this last activity particularly because all too often children leave school with a record of written English that is almost negligible, and in the conditions of modern life that little will soon begin to rust for want of exercise. If they have been encouraged at home from their earliest days to write, what they learn about it in school is likely to be of more lasting value.

These and similar activities I have always found parents very ready to encourage in the child. Arthur's mother, who is one of those who through such participation obtained an astonished insight into how crowded a school day can be, said once: "I can see you teachers really earn your money!"

I wouldn't go that far myself; but I confess it's a nicer thing to hear than that school holidays are too long, teachers' hours too short and their pay-packets too big.